LIVING WITHIN OUR MEANS

LIVING WITHIN OUR MEANS

An Examination of the Argentine Economic Crisis

ALDO FERRER

Translated by Maria-Ines Alvarez
and Nick Caistor

Routledge
Taylor & Francis Group

LONDON AND NEW YORK

First published 1985 by Westview Press

Published 2018 by Routledge
52 Vanderbilt Avenue, New York, NY 10017
2 Park Square, Milton Park, Abingdon, Oxon OX14 4RN

Routledge is an imprint of the Taylor & Francis Group, an informa business

British Cataloguing in Publication Data
Ferrer, Aldo
    Living Within our Means: An Examination of the Argentine Economic
Crisis
    1. Argentinian economic conditions—1945–
    1. Title   2. Third World Foundation
    330.982'064   HC 175
ISBN 13: 978-0-367-00637-2 (hbk)

LC 85-51093

ISBN 13: 978-0-367-15624-4 (pbk)

Contents

Contents

Preface

Argentina's current international insolvency presents it with the dilemma of how to proceed in order to ensure its economic sovereignty; in other words, the right to decide its own destiny. The answer is: for Argentina to try to live within its means. For as long as the present crisis lasts, Argentina must rely on its own resources to overcome it, to get its economy moving again and to regain its international viability.

The basic message contained in these pages is that the crisis goes beyond the social and the economic spheres, however serious these two aspects of it may be. It also involves challenges to the sovereignty of the nation. The choice is clear: the Argentine government can either become simply the administrator of the foreign debt on behalf of the creditor banks or it can regain control of its economy to resolve the crisis by putting national interests first. Nothing more, nothing less. The conclusion is that for real economic and political independence to be possible, the Argentine government has to take the decision to live within its own means, and, once that decision has been taken, to work out its negotiating position with respect to its foreign creditors.

In such a situation, it is hardly surprising that the old argument crops up as to whether Argentina is or is not able to grow using its own resources, relying to a large extent on its internal market. All the traditional questions about Argentina's development are being raised again, but this time at a particularly critical moment. If they wish to be coherent, those who defend the viability of a nationally based development strategy must demonstrate that our resources are sufficient to overcome the crisis and can produce growth. Others preach that Argentina is helpless and that both foreign capital and the international market are essential to accumulation and growth. Their programme was adopted wholeheartedly by the military governments from 1976 to 1983, with results that are now all too obvious.

The danger at present is not one of continuing this orthodox line, which the seven years of military rule have totally discredited. It is rather that Argentines may be incoherent in their attempts to reach the inevitable conclusion: that if they wish to be independent, they must make do with their own resources. The orthodox strategy has left a deep impression, and one often hears representative leaders of Argentine national life insinuating, or even stating openly, that without foreign resources there can be neither development nor a way out of the crisis. If this were really true, there would be no possibility of Argentina being independent, given its current international insolvency.

Fortunately, however, this is not true. Argentina's land area is the eighth largest in the world, it is exceptionally rich in natural resources, has a surplus of foodstuffs and is practically self-sufficient in energy. Its 30 million inhabitants' average earnings are approximately $3000 a year, and it has a savings rate of 20 per cent. It is a society with a high cultural level, a wealth of technological expertise, and no social, ethnic or religious incompatibilities. A society with such advantages does have the necessary resources and capability for development.

This list of objective factors which illustrate Argentina's basic potential and the feasibility of independent development does not imply that an autarkic strategy would be viable. Independence is not autarky, nor does national development mean ignoring the importance of international trade and the links with foreign countries which are an integral part of the current system. What it does imply is that Argentina's economic policy should reflect the objectives of change, social justice and a proper international role which will allow it to achieve its full potential. This will be feasible only if Argentina fully accepts the possibilities of its own potential and refuses to accept the orthodox criteria which are still predominant in international financial circles, criteria that coincide within Argentina with the views held by that sector which is the inheritor of pre-industrial Argentina and has been the wielder of authoritarian power. The defence of Argentine sovereignty calls, first and foremost, for Argentines to sort out their affairs. The present chaos and disorder are so great as to render impossible any attempt at an independent policy.

The second message of this book is that this could be the starting point for the consolidation of the democratic system in Argentina. The very depth of the crisis presents the country with an unavoidable choice: either this marks the end of authoritarian regimes, or Argentina will be plunged headlong into complete dissolution amid unending conflict. The response to this dilemma will be decisive in the future performance of the Argentine economy.

The third point is that the economic crisis cannot be resolved simply by bringing into play the traditional instruments of economic policy and allowing market forces free rein. A basic agreement is needed among the principal sectors of Argentine society to defend democracy and support a coherent policy in order to stimulate the economy, raise the standard of living, bring down inflation and strengthen the country's international position. This has led to the widespread and justified conviction of the need for an Economic and Social Pact to meet the crisis.

Such a Pact, however, would fail if it did not restore order to the economic and financial system. The country's fiscal policy and foreign debt have created massive imbalances in public finances and in the monetary system, which can be seen in the disastrous situation that characterises all the markets and the country's international relations. The constitutional government of President Raúl Alfonsín inherited a bankrupt country, and a State which is almost powerless to reverse the present trends or to resolve the most pressing social tensions. Any economic and social recovery must be based on a thorough financial reform which will restore order to the public sector, the monetary system and the country's international payments.

This book is divided into two parts. Part I proceeds from an examination of the current fiscal chaos and the external debt question, to an identification of the main sources of the present public and monetary imbalances and then outlines some basic measures for resolving the problems. It also proposes an extensive financial reform which would aim to reduce the fiscal deficit and its effects on the money supply to levels compatible with an economic recovery and a drastic cut in the inflation rate. A strategy for paying the public debt is central to this proposed reform. The foreign-debt question is of paramount importance both because of the international aspect of the problem and the difficulty of reconciling the fulfilment of external commitments with the need to revive the Argentine economy and bring price stability. Part I, therefore, begins by looking at the size of the debt problem and the different strategies for meeting it. The current worsening of inflation is seen as a specific means for dealing with the international payments problem within the context of the present Argentine social and political situation. We then turn to proposals for a reform of the financial system, with an outline of the main measures suggested for achieving this. Part I ends with an examination of how Argentina can meet its external financial commitments while still reviving its own economy.

Part II discusses possible policies for meeting the crisis, on the basis of a Pact between the main sectors of Argentine society. The first section pinpoints the basic questions which have to be resolved to facilitate such a Pact. We then examine the situation in which the constitutional government had to elaborate its economic policies, and suggest a strategy for recovery. There follows an explanation of the policies which seem to us necessary in order to produce economic recovery, a cut in inflation, and to ensure that Argentina can meet its international payments. The book ends with a consideration of how the chief macro-economic variables will be affected if the proposed policies are put into effect, taking into consideration the current situation.

A preliminary version of the proposals discussed in this book was presented at the Centro de Estudios de Coyuntura del Instituto de Desarrollo Economico y Social in Buenos Aires. The exchange of ideas on that occasion enabled me to broaden its scope and to arrive at more definite conclusions for whose accuracy I am entirely responsible.

Aldo Ferrer
Buenos Aires, November 1983

Part I

Financial reform: from a default on payments to a viable Argentina

1

A bankrupt economy, a shackled country: the epilogue of monetarism

The regime and the economic policies which were born with the March 1976 *coup d'état* in Argentina ended with galloping inflation and generalised disorder that threatened complete economic breakdown. The reasons for this outcome of military rule lie in both the productive and financial sectors. In the productive sector, they are linked to the decline in production, levels of employment, and the standard of living of the population. In the financial sector, the reasons can be found in the foreign debt, fiscal chaos, and the over-importance of the role played by domestic financial intermediaries.

The productive and financial sides of the economy are of course closely interrelated. A revival of economic activity and an increase in the standard of living would lead to a reduction in the financial imbalances. However, it is impossible to mobilise spare capacity and return to growth without restoring order to the financial sector. This latter is indispensable if two of the preconditions for economic recovery are to be met: namely, cutting the inflation rate drastically and readjusting Argentina's balance-of-payments situation so that its economy becomes viable again internationally.

The current problems are especially serious for the impact they have on the welfare and expectations of Argentine society. They are also disturbing because they bring Argentina into conflict with the international private banking system, because of the virtual suspension of foreign-debt payments. The way in which the country's international insolvency is handled is of the utmost importance. On it will depend which economic strategy is adopted for dealing with the crisis and, at a more fundamental level, will determine whether or not Argentina still has the elementary right of a sovereign country to decide its own destiny.

In this book we uphold the view that a sweeping financial reform is necessary to enable the Argentine economy to recover, to regain control over the economic process, and to re-establish its international viability. Argentina's fiscal and monetary chaos must be sorted out if the country is to negotiate payment of the foreign debt on terms compatible with its economic sovereignty. The question therefore is not whether to undertake a radical readjustment or not. The question is *how* this radical change is to be carried out, and who is to make the decisions. The alternative to this would be a continuation of the present chaos, and an unthinkable future.

A few examples will suffice to give some idea of the seriousness of Argentina's financial imbalances and international insolvency. The interest payments alone on the foreign debt currently represent 60 per cent of the value of Argentina's exports, close to 8 per cent of GDP, and 70 per cent of net savings. These interest payments absorb the investment capacity of all national savings. Argentina cannot pay the interest on its foreign debt without refinancing most of it. Amortisation payments are equivalent to twice the current value of exports and will have to be rescheduled in their entirety.

In the public sector, the present deficit is appoximately 15 per cent of GDP. Since monetary resources represent altogether some 13 per cent of GDP, and the State has to seek the rest through credit from the Central Bank, this deficit doubles the means of payment and lends further impetus to the rise in prices.* Finally, the fall of the economy's rate of monetisation and the disproportionate growth of financial institutions and allied companies have led to dealers' costs that amount to approximately 20 per cent of every peso lent. If we make an international comparison, the Bank of America has deposits ten times as

* In an economy where monetary assets represent only a small proportion of the total capital stock and of private savings, the public sector borrowing requirement cannot be met by purchasing private monetary assets. In such a situation, public expenditure can only be financed by taxing real income or by 'inflationary tax' through the expansion of money. The latter is what occurs in Argentina.

large as the whole Argentine financial system, and yet only half the staff. Even if the inflation rate were nil, and the borrowing rate also nil, the lending rate would need to be in the order of 20 per cent simply to pay the costs of the financial intermediaries. This being the case, the State has lost control of the economy. It cannot regulate exchange rates, the interest rate, the fiscal deficit or monetary supply. In such a state of affairs, to speak of 'economic policy' is an abuse of language. The behaviour of the economy is governed by the extraordinary fiscal and monetary imbalances, in which servicing the foreign debt plays a major part.

The government lacks the means to control total demand, production, or prices. Any attempt to revive the economy is immediately nullified by greater price increases. The state-run enterprises face a serious financial imbalance, because of their foreign debts. Between 1970 and 1974, the cost of servicing that debt represented 12 per cent of their sales; by 1983 this had risen to over 50 per cent. Such a situation makes the objective of boosting productivity and reducing costs unattainable; fiscal policy is powerless in the face of the existing huge deficit.

The same is true of monetary policy. The fiscal deficit and its effects on the monetary system make such a high level of money supply necessary that the inflationary process is fuelled and this in turn hinders any attempt to direct credit or to reduce the interest rate. Trying to reduce the cost of money and to increase credit to the private sector immediately leads to new price rises and a fresh outburst of speculation against the peso. The economic agents have such negative expectations that any attempt to stimulate the economy by fiscal and monetary policy leads to a prior upward adjustment of prices, combined with capital flight. Argentina's exchange policy is also severely affected by the imbalance which the foreign debt causes. In spite of consistent trade balance surplus, the exchange rate has to be adjusted to restrict imports. When the peso is overvalued, the external imbalance is made still worse, and forces an increase in the interest rate as a last means of adjustment. However, when there is no confidence whatsoever in financial circles, speculation against the peso will continue, no matter how high the rate of interest. In such a situation, the peso loses its position as a deposit currency or money of account. The 'dollarisation' of transactions becomes more and more widespread.

The 1976–83 military regime bequeathed an insolvent economy and a disastrous economic and social situation to the constitutional government. It has left a public sector that is overwhelmed by fiscal and monetary difficulties and the burden of foreign payments, and finds itself in a position where it is almost powerless to reverse the trends of economic life. The return of democracy under a civilian president is not in itself enough to guarantee a change in the course of these events. The government must regain control of economic policy and eliminate the basic fiscal and monetary imbalances. One of the measures needed is a realistic approach to the foreign-debt service payment. This will help Argentina out of its current insolvency and will re-establish the conditions for the Argentine economy's international viability.

2

A strategy for the payment of foreign-debt interest

In order to discuss the financial reform needed to restore order to the Argentine economy, we need first to analyse the effect of foreign-debt interest payments on the public sector and the balance of payments.

If we consider first the public sector, two things should be borne in mind. First, that US$30,000 million out of a total foreign debt of US$ 40,000 million is owed by the public sector. In addition, approximately half of the US$10,000 million owed by the private sector is guaranteed by the State. Secondly, that the interest payments on the foreign debt represent a substantial proportion of total public spending. As an indication, these interest payments represented, in the five years 1970–74, a mere 1 per cent of consolidated public sector expenditure and 0.4 per cent of GDP, whereas in 1982 the figures were 17 per cent and 6 per cent respectively.

The foreign-debt problem is therefore largely concentrated in the public sector and chiefly revolves around interest payments. In reality, Argentina cannot pay off any of the capital on its debts and, in the present state of affairs, the creditor banks need only to recoup the interest on their loans. According to the regulations existing in the world's financial centres, a loan may be kept on a bank's account for as long as the interest payments on it have been received. If this is not the case, it has to be counted as a loss, consequently reducing the lending agency's capital or necessitating the use of reserves. In the United States, banks registered in New York State can only claim as performing assets those accounts on which the interest payments are not more than three months in arrears, since these banks must present their books to the monetary authorities every quarter. For banks registered in other states, the maximum

6

delay period is six months. The banks' main problem therefore is to ensure that they receive regular payment on the interest so that they may classify them as performing assets.

Interest payments on the foreign debt cannot simply be covered by a transfer of funds from the entire Argentine population to those who made loans to the public sector. This transfer has to be made outside the country, and consequently has to be counterbalanced by a surplus in international payments to Argentina. If we imagine, to simplify the analysis, that it is the private sector which carries out all international transactions then, for the system as a whole to balance, the savings the State must make on its overall operations to fulfil the interest payments on the public foreign debt must be exactly the same as the private sector international transactions surplus.

A surplus on the current account balance of payments means that the private sector is generating more funds from exports and other means than it needs for its imports and other expenditure abroad. Thus the foreign operations of the private sector lead to monetary expansion. The State has to absorb this increase in liquidity by means of a saving between its total income and expenditure and/or by increasing its indebtedness to the private sector. In short, it must seek to reduce domestic consumer and investment demand to the level of the goods and services available after payment of the foreign-debt interest. The State has to absorb the increased liquidity generated by the surplus in the private sector's international transactions, and to cut salaries and profits to be in a position to meet the interest payments. If it cannot do this, then the economic system will have an excess of funds in the private sector and liquidity which is too high for the goods and services available. In this case, an increase in prices and a devaluation of exchange rates is inevitable.

With this in mind, two alternative ways of rescheduling the debt interest payments can be envisaged. The first, which we might qualify as *stabilising*, is the one in which the State seeks the resources it needs in the private sector. The second, or *inflationary* way, is to reduce real wages and firms' profits, and to discourage internal demand and imports by increasing the interest rate and the exchange rate of the peso.

We will examine first the details of the non-inflationary solution, then turn our attention to the inflationary way, which is the one which currently exists in Argentina.

3

A stabilising programme to deal with the foreign debt

There will have to be an extraordinary turn-around in public sector accounts if the foreign-debt interest is to be paid without any fiscal deficit. At the moment, this deficit represents 15 per cent of GDP, of which 6 per cent corresponds to the outstanding interest on the foreign debt, and 9 per cent to the deficit from the public sector's other operations. This latter is well-nigh equivalent to total public investment. In other words, for 1983 current savings in the public sector (current income minus current expenditure) are close to zero. To cancel the public sector deficit, one would have to transform the 9 per cent deficit arising from overall public sector operations to a surplus of 6 per cent, which could be used to pay the foreign-debt interest and to operate with balanced books. This means that public sector savings would have to expand from almost nil in 1983 to 15 per cent of GDP, which implies a level of public saving unprecedented in Argentina's financial history. How could such a radical transformation in public sector operations be accomplished?

The answer lies in increasing income (in other words, by increasing taxes and the real prices of public services) and in reducing expenditure. The cuts in expenditure could be made chiefly in spending on security and defence. A reduction in military expenditure could contribute up to 4 per cent of GDP, making this move essential, whatever economic policy is adopted. The minimum level of public investment required to complete the public works pro-gramme already begun is at least 7 per cent of GDP, so that reducing expenditure in this area could not contribute more than 2 per cent of GDP. The other 9 per cent needed if the foreign-debt interest payments are to be met without causing a deficit, would have to come from other cuts in expenditure (wages, etc.) and by increasing tax contributions. That is, further reductions in consumption and in private investment would be needed in order to balance the fiscal accounts.

Let us turn now to the modification needed in the balance of payments. In order to simplify our analysis, we will continue to consider only the question of how to deal with the interest payments on the foreign debt which, in 1983, reached something in the region of US$4,000 million. However, a more realistic approach would mean that we have to take into account the US$1,000 million interest due on private foreign debt. In fact, a considerable readjustment of international payments has already taken place, thanks to a sizeable reduction in imports. This cut has only been made possible because of a continuing depressed level of domestic economic activity. This readjustment is not enough in itself. The current account surplus would have to double if the debt interest payments were to be covered.

To achieve this, either exports must be boosted, and/or imports restricted. A boost in exports is only partially achievable by changing Argentina's economic policies. Supply from the agricultural sector and the exportable surplus produced depend, to some extent, on the weather. In the short term, the sector's capacity to respond to better relative prices is limited.

Any possibility of increasing the export of manufactured goods has been greatly hampered by the dismantling of Argentina's industrial capacity during the past few years. Above all, the most important factor affecting the possibility of increasing exports is the behaviour of the world market. Protectionism in the industrialised nations (as in the case of the EEC's common agricultural policy), subsidies offered to boost the export of domestic production (as in the case of cereals in the United States), and the sensitivity of terms of exchange to any alteration in world demand, all act to create strict limits and unstable conditions for Argentina's exports. Given the situation in Argentina as regards the supply of exportable goods, and the state of the international market, any rise in the exchange rate can have only a slight influence on exports. To sum up, the possibility of increasing the surplus on international payments by increasing exports is limited, at least in the short term.

This means that the necessary surplus must be found chiefly by reducing imports. There is only a small possibility of achieving this by import substitution. On the one hand, Argentina's industrial capacity has been hard hit and, at least in the short term, there can be little hope that domestic industrial production could recover sufficiently to produce import substitutes. On the other, the import coefficient in Argentina is already low (in the region of 10 per cent of GDP) and, however wholehearted the effort at import substitution might be, imports tend to grow more quickly than GDP. The most optimistic estimates put the relation of imports to GDP at around 1:3. In addition, since the changes necessary in the public sector would bring about a further reduction in internal demand, one could expect industrial activity to contract still further. This implies a further limit to the possibilities of responding to any stimulus for import substitution which might arise if there were an increase in effective exchange rates, and a subsequent increase in the protection of the domestic market.

All this means, therefore, that any increase in the surplus on international transactions needed to meet the foreign-debt interest payments is unlikely to come from any boost in exports or from import substitution. It will have to come from a fresh contraction of imports, arising from a further decline in internal economic activity. The modifications demanded by the payment of interest on the foreign debt present insurmountable problems for the formulation of economic policies in Argentina. On the one hand, they presuppose the creation of an extraordinary surplus between domestic production and levels of consumption and investment, and the conversion of this surplus into currency. On the other, the creation of this surplus and its transfer out of the country would have a negative effect on production and employment, and would steadily increase the relative cost of any such modification. This second tendency would be reflected by a drop in real wages and in the private investment needed to create the surplus. This in turn would deflate overall demand and levels of economic activity. In addition, any reduction in imports would lead to a drop in industrial production to bring it into line with the lower supply levels of imported inputs.

This is an extreme case of the consequences of the orthodox view put forward by the International Monetary Fund (IMF). Its aim is to achieve the necessary adjustment in the allocation of resources and the balance of payments to facilitate the debt interest payments in a situation where prices are stable. The problem is that this objective produces a drastic fall in living standards and negative transfers of income in the attempt to improve the relative price of exportable production. It also encourages an accelerated contraction of both production and employment. It is plain that, even if the first of these consequences were politically acceptable, the second would make such a policy unsustainable in the medium and long term.

The IMF's orthodox formula would perhaps be viable if the adjustment strategy included a refinancing of the payable interest. The debtor nations ought, in any case, to reduce imports of goods and services in line with the limits set by their exports. But this refinancing would make the economic adjustment much less painful than is currently the case, when the payment of all or a large part of the interest due implies, as in Argentina, an unprecedented fall in living standards and the prolonged contraction of both production and employment. The IMF at present does not have sufficient resources to enable it to resolve the debtor countries' problems and refinance the interest payable. Its total funds are something less than US$100,000 million, whereas the foreign debt of the developing countries is approximately US$600,000 million and the annual interest payable close to US$60,000 million. The necessary resources will have to be provided, therefore, by the international private banking system but, given the present critical situation, these banks are seeking to reduce their net loan position and recuperate at least the interest due them. Also, given the interest rate level on the international markets, to increase the volume of debt as quickly as has been the case over the past few years would mean an excessive growth of liabilities, which have already reached levels that are impossible for the debtor countries to pay.

For Argentina and the other main debtors, this orthodox strategy poses insoluble problems, which manifest themselves in Argentina in the present economic chaos and inflationary explosion.

4

The inflationary way of dealing with the foreign debt

Whatever the circumstances, and in any part of the globe, it would be a mammoth task to reduce living standards so much as to produce a surplus of 6 per cent of GDP and the necessary equivalent in foreign currency to transfer these resources out of the country. In Argentina's case, this task is made even more difficult by the context in which such a considerable effort is being demanded. A few examples will suffice to provide a general picture. In 1983, per capita income was 15 per cent below that of 1975, and the real average was 30 per cent lower. Unemployment and underemployment affected 15 per cent of the workforce; the number of jobs in the manufacturing sector is on a par with the situation thirty years ago. Industry is experiencing its longest and deepest recession in living memory: the physical volume of industrial production is no higher than that fifteen years ago. Idle capacity in industry is around 40 per cent, and in the construction sector as high as 50 per cent.

It is impossible to try to apply an orthodox economic recovery programme in these circumstances. How in fact does the Argentine economy respond to policies which aim at paying the interest on the foreign debt?

The State cannot generate the surplus needed to achieve this, and consequently operates with a substantial deficit that includes the interest on the debt plus the shortfall accruing from the other transactions undertaken by the public sector.

Since there is no domestic capital market, and the system functions at a very low rate of monetisation, the fiscal deficit has to be financed by an expansion of credit from the Central Bank. This creates an extraordinary increase in money supply. It is worth noting just what proportions this montisation of the fiscal deficit would reach. Currently, the coefficient of liquidity (M2/GDP) is approximately 13 per cent. Let us look at the monetary effect of a deficit of 10 per cent financed by the Central Bank. This implies increasing the money supply (M2 = money and banknotes held by the public, plus current account and fixed-term account deposits) by 77 per cent. However, with the present fiscal deficit, and given the current monetary set-up, the overall increase in M2 would be 310 per cent. The monetary system is at present operating with a reserve rate of close to 100 per cent. Since the Central Bank's discount rate for the banks to finance the private sector grows at the same rate as interest, and the banks receive the interest payments from the private sector on behalf of the Central Bank, there is no net increase in the money supply. The growth in liquidity attributable to the bank rate is cancelled out by the private sector's interest payments. However, the Central Bank has to match the borrowing rate of the deposit accounts in private and official banks. These deposits represent 70 per cent of M2 and 9 per cent of GDP. With a borrowing rate of 10 per cent, the money control account which includes these interest payments made by the Central Bank, implies an increase in monetary resources (M2) of 130 per cent. The initial monetary expansion needed to finance the public sector's deficit, plus the money control account, go to make up the more than 300 per cent rise in M2.

It is worth noting that the same results would be obtained with a fractionary reserve system. If this reserve were only 10 per cent of deposits, and M2 was 13 per cent of GDP, the monetary base (money and banknotes in circulation, plus the deposits of financial establishments in the Central Bank) would be equivalent to 3·3 per cent of GDP. In other words, the credit multiplier would be 4. In this case, a 10 per cent deficit in GDP would imply a 300 per cent expansion of the monetary base, which would be passed on, through the credit multiplying factor, to monetary resources (M2).

As the public sector cannot, in practice, generate the surplus to enable payment of the interest on the foreign debt without incurring a deficit or monetary expansion, this foreign debt becomes an important destabilising factor. Net monetary expansion is in fact registered through the private sector. The Central Bank credit which the government uses to make the debt interest payments is absorbed when the public sector buys foreign currency for transfer abroad. However, the external surplus made by the private sector (the excess of income from exports and other items as against the demand for foreign currency to pay for imports and other expenditure) will have caused a net expansion in the money supply that will not have been absorbed by the public sector.

In fact, since the transfer abroad of interest payments on the foreign debt in 1983 was less than the interest due, net monetary expansion is not the same as might be deduced from the relation of interest payments due on the debt to GDP through the fiscal accounts.

The discrepancy lies in refinancing the debt servicing, and delayed payments. Be that as it may, the interest payments actually made on the foreign public debt and their corollary, the surplus gained on foreign transactions by the private sector, have caused an unacceptably high monetary expansion.

When the State lacks the political power to meet its external financial commitments without increasing liquidity, inflation becomes the necessary tool for any change. This creates a sort of inflationary tax, seen in the fall in real wages, profitability in the business and industrial sector, and less money available for the population as a whole. If this is still not enough to restrict imports and generate the necessary balance of payments, an increase in the interest rate and in the exchange rate of the peso are further steps taken to discourage private demand. The leap in the inflation rate in Argentina can be taken as a sign of the imposition of this kind of strategy at a time when much of society is increasingly adamant in its refusal to tolerate any attempt to reduce its real income.

5

The spreading of inflation

The inflation caused by the attempt to pay the foreign-debt interest will set in motion a cumulative process that is bound to add to the pressure originally created by the foreign debt, the fiscal deficit, and monetary growth. As the rate of inflation increases, so further inflationary pressures are created. Chief among these are:

1) A worsening of the fiscal situation due to the fall in the collectable tax revenues, an increasing falling behind in the collection of taxes as compared to price rises, and an increasing gap between fiscal earnings and expenditure. These tendencies affect the public sector's capacity for self-financing and increase its working deficit. In Argentina's recent experience, it can be seen that the relation between tax revenues and expenditure by the Treasury has dropped from 68 per cent in 1979 to 43 per cent in 1983. Furthermore, the depreciation of the peso has increased the value in national currency terms of the foreign currency needed to service the debt and, consequently, the effect of that debt on total expenditure for the public sector and for the fiscal deficit.

2) A rise in the inflation rate and the worsening of the peso's exchange rate produces drastic changes in relative prices and income distribution. This leads to an intensification in the struggle for distribution among the different economic and social sectors, and thereby becomes a further factor in the inflationary process. In addition, the drop in the population's real income and in the goods and services available leads to efforts by each group to force other sectors to absorb the costs of this adjustment. The struggle for distribution becomes even more intense.

3) A rise in the inflation rate leads to increasing pessimism in economic circles, which aggravates the inflationary tendency. This leads to pre-emptive price rises and a greater instability in the labour market. The parallel exchange market becomes a reliable indicator of how little confidence key sectors have, and the growing devaluation of the peso only adds to the instability.

This worsening in the economic situation and the increasing inflationary pressure are also shown in other ways. Given the limits on credit expansion imposed under any IMF agreement, the monetary growth needed to pay for the fiscal deficit absorbs the greater part of the permitted credit that has been created. Since the system itself cannot even meet the interest payments due, it is the private sector which must generate alternative means of finance. This leads to the creation of credit chains between firms and the increasing use of credit such as post-dated cheques. According to some estimates, this non-bank economic circuit accounts for approximately half of the M2 of total institutional finance in Argentina. In this non-bank economy, interest rates have reached unheard of levels, such as 40 per cent per month! This tendency in the financial sector leads to an increase in firms' costs and restricts the levels of private consumption and investment. It also adds to the risk involved in financial transactions, since there are no longer any institutional intermediaries to guarantee the lines of credit.

These tendencies have other effects on the financial sector. The increase in the rate of inflation leads to a drop in the real liquidity of the system as a whole. During the period of military government from 1976 to 1983, the coefficient of liquidity (M2/GDP) reached its highest in 1980 at 25 per cent. Ever since then, the rate has steadily declined, despite the increase in the money supply rate. Since the inflation rate was always higher, real liquidity fell. The smaller real volume of banking operations has increased the effect of operating costs and made still more disproportionate the role of the financial sector. It has also caused a flow of deposits towards institutions considered as more secure such as official or foreign banks, and the large national ones with private capital. A large number of medium-sized and small financial institutions are operating with a rate of third-party deposits to capital that is wholly inadequate for their proper functioning and profitability. The Central Bank has to intervene with special credit facilities to prevent bankruptcy and the official banks have had to use the call mechanism to shore up organisations whose deposits were less than their asset portfolios. The increase in inflationary pressure has thus hit the financial sector particularly hard.

In spite of the harshness of the economic adjustment being undertaken, and the size of the trade balance surplus generated in order to meet the debt service payments, there has been no accompanying climate of confidence in Argentina's viability either amongst local agents or amongst the foreign creditors. The fiscal deficit, inflation, and social tension paint a highly unstable picture. In such circumstances, the creditor banks try to recover as much as they can, push their commission and interest rates as high as possible, seek to limit any negotiated refinancing to the shortest period possible, and insist on reducing the amounts they have on loan, thus denying sources of additional credit which would help to alleviate the foreign payments situation and permit recovery in production and employment.

Consequently, seeking to service the foreign debt by using inflation as a mechanism leads to the worst of all possible worlds: a drop in real income and in living standards, spiralling inflation, increasing lack of confidence, and relentless pressure from the foreign creditors.

The structuralist analysis of inflation makes the distinction between fundamental inflationary pressures and these mechanisms which spread it. The former are those which cause the original rise in prices. The latter are those which spread these initial pressures through the whole of the system. In Argentina's current experience, the fundamental factor which explains the huge rise in the inflation rate is the accumulated imbalance in the public sector, the balance of payments, and the cost of financial intermediaries. Another way of describing this same factor might be to say that the State is incapable of carrying out a truly non-inflationary settlement by means of a surplus in fiscal operations and in the balance of payments. All the other factors are mechanisms which spread inflation: the devaluations of the peso, the fight for the distribution of income, the rise in interest rates, constant increases in public service charges, and so on.

6

Financial reform

Never before in its history has Argentina experienced a situation to compare with the present one. The crisis of the 1930s was different in scale and character. Then, the foreign debt was in public bonds, not in the banking sector. The response, however, did include such extreme measures as control of the exchange rate, the restriction of imports, a moratorium on debt payments and, in the end, freeing of the economy to meet the unpaid debts. Internationally, the experience which perhaps most closely mirrors that of contemporary Argentina was that of Germany at the end the two world wars. Germany could not meet the reparations demanded by the Treaty of Versailles after World War I, and this led to France and Belgium occupying the Ruhr in 1923, followed by the collapse of the German mark in that same year. When the German government attempted to buy foreign currency on the exchange market, it caused an uncontrollable devaluation of the mark. It is interesting to note that the impossibility of meeting the reparations was to some extent a result of the demands made by the victors in the war. They continued to impose measures against German exports and promoted sales of their own goods within Germany, thus preventing Germany achieving the surplus it needed to meet its commitments. Argentina and the other debtor nations of today are in a somewhat similar situation. They face severe conditions for the payment of their debts, while at the same time the industrial countries' protectionism, subsidies to their own exports, and the deterioration in the terms of trade, lead to a drop in export earnings for the debtor nations, and a consequent reduction in the surplus on their foreign payments. The situation in Germany changed dramatically after 1924 with the application of the Dawes Plan. Under this, German reparations were paid for by means of fresh credits supplied by the victorious countries. Between 1924 and 1931, Germany paid 11,100 million marks in reparations, and increased its foreign debt with new credits totalling 18,000 million marks. In other words, there was a net transfer of resources to Germany rather than a negative flow, which would have been more in line with the demands made by the victor nations. The crisis of the 1930s and the rise of Nazism brought this experiment to a close.

Germany's experience after World War II is also worthy of note. In June 1948, the occupying forces from the US, France and Britain carried out a monetary reform which consisted of a repudiation of the Reich's public foreign debt, the confiscation of 90 per cent of the money supply (money in circulation and private deposit), combined with a simultaneous derogation of 90 per cent of the financial debts owed by individuals to the banking system. In this way Germany eliminated both public and private debt and its service payments, which had been crippling any hope of economic revival or of fiscal and monetary reform. It should be noted that the debt which was cancelled in this way belonged to the Germans themselves, and that the measures were introduced in a country controlled by occupying forces. Be that as it may, such a reform was necessary to pave the way for the reconstruction and subsequent growth of the German economy.

These examples will serve to show just how great a challenge Argentina is now facing. Decisions taken now will affect the country's future for many years. They cannot be properly taken unless and until Argentina recovers its ability to decide for itself and is able to control its own economic policies. The crisis is so grave that there can be no compromise solution with regard to this basic question: is Argentina a country which decides its own destiny or isn't it?

Three crucial measures must be taken if Argentina is to regain control over its economy:

1) It must reduce the fiscal deficit by means of the following

immediate measures: a refinancing of the interest payments on the foreign debt which the country cannot meet;
a reduction in security and defence costs to their historical
average (2 per cent of GDP); and an effort to boost tax
revenues. Taken together, these three steps would generate
resources equivalent to approximately 10 per cent of GDP.
On this basis, the rest of public expenditure and other tax
revenues could be directed in a way which would ensure
that the policy of economic recovery and control of inflation
were successful.

2) It should carry out stringent economies in the use of
available foreign currency by the application of a rigorous
control on essential imports and on payments to service
and capital accounts. For as long as the emergency lasts,
Argentina must resolve to pay its way, i.e. to limit the
demand for foreign currency to the amount generated by
export earnings, less acceptable interest payments on the
foreign debt. In the short term, these interest payments
could not exceed approximately 10 per cent of the value of
exports, plus a higher percentage (approximately 20 per
cent) on their annual increase. This last measure would tie
Argentina's ability to pay its foreign debt to a resurgence in
world trade. The current level of exports and their probable
growth, in an economy which is practically self-sufficient in
energy and a net exporter of foodstuffs, is sufficient to allow
the imports of essential services and goods which cannot be
produced domestically. Neither Argentina nor any other of
the other major debtor nations should experience a net
increase in their debt position, whatever economic policy
they follow, that is, a deficit on the balance-of-payments
current account which would have to be met by fresh
foreign credit. The problem Argentina is facing is not
whether it is possible to obtain further credit from abroad,
but to decide just how much it can pay of the interest on its
present debt without stifling an economic recovery. This is
the inevitable situation in the short term.

3) It must aim to reduce the size of the financial sector in
order to cut its operating costs. The present operating cost
of 20 per cent of performing assets must be brought down,

in the first place, to 8 per cent. This contraction of the system implies cutting the number of institutions and subsidiaries, getting rid of unnecessary staff, and the introduction of regulations which would lead to technical savings (the rate of third-party resources to internal capital, etc.) essential to the proper functioning of the system. In order to facilitate this reform and to minimise its social effects, adequate payment should be made to the personnel made redundant, and outline plans be drawn up for whatever transformation, closure or regrouping of the financial institutions involved be deemed necessary.

These three basic decisions imply a profound fiscal and monetary reform, as well as a re-examination of the foreign payments question. Argentina is faced with a situation that is typical of a country which has emerged from a war with its productive apparatus and its fiscal and financial systems destroyed. That is why Argentina is urgently in need of a post-war strategy to resolve its crisis. Europe's revival after 1945 would have been impossible without the far-reaching fiscal and monetary reforms that were carried out.

The German 'economic miracle' (*Wirtschaftswunder*) is based on the 1948 monetary and financial reform. The current situation in Argentina is somewhat different since, for example, the origin of our debt is foreign, whereas in Germany it was domestic. However, a wide-ranging financial reform adapted to the situation in Argentina is equally necessary if we are to overcome the crisis and free the forces of economic growth.

The reform measures proposed assume a solid political backing for Argentina's constitutional government and aim to make those interests and structures which are responsible for the imbalance absorb the cost. As with the financial reforms undertaken after the war in Europe, there should be no reduction in real wages or in employment. On the contrary, the forces of growth and accumulation would be released immediately, so that employment and real levels of income would rise. That is not to say that this policy will be easy to achieve politically. Any attempt to reduce military expenditure, or to raise the question of how foreign-debt payments are to be met, or to increase taxes on those sectors with the highest incomes, demand a broadly based political backing as well as a clear-sighted and responsible use of the main instruments of economic policy. The adjustment we are proposing is vital to restore order to the Argentine economy. It is, furthermore, the only one which is politically possible in the current situation of disarray and social tension.

On this basis, it will be possible to reach the goals which Argentine society is seeking: to raise the standard of living, to get rid of inflation, to resume growth, and to create a new climate of confidence which will sweep away the current pessimism and despair. Such a reform is also essential to provide the basis for the following decisions:

1) To direct credit into desired areas, and to reduce real interest rates in order to stimulate the use of spare productive capacity and to allow the formation of reproductive capital to start again. To use tax revenues and public sector expenditure in order to improve education and health services, provide greater resources for house building and connected infrastructure, and to redistribute income more in line with criteria of social equality. To control effective exchange and import duty rates in order to promote exports, to strengthen the country's industrial capacity, and to promote Argentina's ability for innovation and technological change. Without a prior financial reform all the political objectives, called for by both business and labour organisations, would remain as unachievable dreams. The vicious circle of hyper-inflation and the shrinking of the Argentine economy would destroy any possibility of reversing the current tendencies.

2) An agreed compromise must be reached in the struggle for the distribution of the national income between the various sectors of society. This compromise would have to be sustained for as long as the economic emergency persists. There is general agreement that such a Pact is an essential instrument with which to fight the crisis. However, any such Pact would be doomed to rapid failure if the causes of the hyper-inflation and the destruction of wealth

were not rooted out. That is to say, if it were not preceded by financial reform.

Argentina is emerging from a war waged over a period of eight years by monetarism against the country's most important structures, in which its productive system was badly hit, and a fiscal and monetary imbalance created which has rendered ineffective all attempts by the State to re-orient the economy. The constitutional government should not be under any illusion as to the seriousness of the crisis it has to resolve.

7

Negotiating the foreign debt

The strategy adopted for paying Argentina's foreign debt is of central importance to the financial reform which in turn is necessary for resolving the country's crisis. The constitutional government has not been elected to pursue an orthodox monetarist path. They must not even attempt to follow this course. Nor must they continue to encourage hyper-inflation as a way of meeting the country's foreign commitments.

The constitutional government will have to undertake a sweeping financial reform to resolve the crisis and, once this has been carried out, must seek new negotiating terms for dealing with its foreign creditors. Economic policy should be decided in the country's own decisionmaking centres, as a demonstration of the right to self-determination of a sovereign nation. If this policy were formulated as a result of hasty negotiations with the IMF, Argentina would find itself in the role of merely administering its foreign debt on behalf of the international banking system. The first thing the government must do is to make up its own mind about what economic policy it is to follow, then seek to strengthen its position with the widest support possible from the country's political and social groups. Only when this political decision has been taken, can it begin negotiations with its foreign creditors.

The constitutional government has inherited a bankrupt country, a country unable to pay the interest due on its foreign debt according to the initially agreed terms. This crisis has three main causes: the policies followed by the military regimes between 1976 and 1983, the rashness with which the creditor banks lent money to Argentina unconditionally, and the deterioration of the international situation (interest rates, terms of trade, restrictions on world trade, etc). All of these factors have affected Argentina's ability to pay its external debts.

A recognition of the present facts must be the starting point for devising a strategy that enables Argentina to meet its international commitments. The foreign financial debt should be considered apart from all the other economic variables, in other words, from the budget for the State and the state-run enterprises, and from the balance-of-payments accounts. Administration of the debt should be the exclusive responsibility of the Executive.* Since the funds available for the payment of the foreign debt would be considerably less than the interest payments due, the rest, plus amortisation payments, would have to be refinanced. Unless this were done, the sums unpaid would accumulate. In this case, a decision would have to be taken as to how this increase in debt was categorised until Argentina's ability to pay off its foreign debt had improved, and/or a rescheduling plan was worked out that would ensure that the overdue sums are paid. The trade debt should be considered separately from the financial one, and no postponement of the former should be allowed, in order to avoid any problems in the flow of trade. Argentina's debt problem is essentially of a financial nature rather than one of international trade.

The situation created by Argentina's insolvency is certain to cause serious differences with the international financial community and the IMF. These latter strongly support the view that the debtor countries should pay off all interest on loans and make a commitment with their creditors, through the IMF, to follow an economic policy that aims at generating the necessary surplus of resources to achieve this. The current agreements the IMF is negotiating with Argentina, Brazil, Mexico and others imply an overall strategy which subordinates economic policy to orthodox criteria for dealing with the problem.

The present foreign payments crisis which Argentina

* With the exception of the private foreign debt which is not guaranteed by the State, accounting for approximately 10 per cent of Argentina's total foreign debt. Transfer abroad of the service payments on this debt would also be conditional on the availability of foreign currency.

and other countries are facing is different from those of the 1950s and 1960s. On those occasions, the problems were closely linked to transitory situations, and the deficits could be dealt with thanks to short-term plans which generated a surplus in international payments. Agreements made at that time with the IMF committed the national economies only for a limited period of time, and did not imply that the direction those economies took, and their place in the international order, would be decided for an indefinite period to come. The problem arising now is different in essence. The debts are so huge that the refinancing agreements and the links with the IMF will be much longer term. It follows that, at a more profound level, what is in question is the right of the debtor countries to decide their own destiny; in other words, their own idea of development and their relation to the international order. The old wish for hegemony of the international power centres is making a disguised re-appearance in the serious question of foreign debt. But the terms involved have changed. Social and political tensions, plus the size of the main debtor countries, means that they cannot be subordinated, indefinitely, to the orthodox criteria which govern international financial thinking. To insist on these criteria would lead to insoluble conflicts between the debtors and their creditors, and cause social and political unrest that would threaten the stability of the entire world order.

Beyond these considerations, there is very little rationality behind these orthodox viewpoints. It is undeniably true that these nations contracted their debt because of a lamentable management of international payments. The clearest example of this is Argentina, where the debt with foreign banks increased sevenfold between 1975 and 1981, whilst GDP growth was nil. But this is not the whole story. Throughout the 1970s, the international banks were anxious to place their surplus liquid assets, and they found new clients among the main developing countries, particularly within Latin America. Argentina's debt, together with that of Brazil and Mexico, makes up close to 50 per cent of the total international banking debt of non oil-exporting developing countries. The banks were willing to commit disproportionate amounts of their own resources, with no guarantees whatsoever, to finance such irresponsible and damaging economic policies as those followed in Argentina and Chile. The experience does not seem to have made the banks any wiser in their operations. Now that the crisis has broken, they are trying to fleece the debtor countries by making them pay commissions, spreads, and other charges for the refinancing operations which, in more responsible circles within the United States and Europe, are regarded as scandalously extortionate. In this respect, it is interesting to consult the debate in the US House of Representatives on the Reagan Administration's plan to increase the US quota in the IMF.

It is also clear that the policies adopted by the world's industrial centres are designed to restrict the export capacity of the debtor countries. Protectionism by the EEC, the US and the other industrialised nations; the high interest rates which are a consequence of US monetary and fiscal policy; the slump in world trade and in the terms of trade for primary goods, all tend to hit the debtor countries' exports and weaken their ability to fulfil foreign financial commitments.

Therein lies the irrationality at the heart of the IMF and the international financial community's thinking which aims to make the whole weight of repayment fall upon the debtor countries, when they are in fact responsible for only part of the problem. Argentina or Brazil might succeed in paying for their own errors, but not those of the creditor banks or of US policy as well. It is important to recognise the true situation before it is too late. In the 1930s, when the multilateral system of trade and payments collapsed, the cost of reconstructing it was shared between debtors and creditors. The external financial debt consisted mainly of public bonds which depreciated with the international crisis. Redeeming these bonds, at a price lower than their issue cost, meant in effect that the creditors were taking on themselves part of the burden of the crisis and of the settlement of international payments. This time, however, almost all the debt is in the banking sector, and the creditors apparently wish to recoup all the interest and the capital that they loaned, as well as adding extra charges beyond and above the cost of money in the international markets. This position is clearly untenable.

A number of analysts, politicians, and even spokesmen for the financial sector in the United States and Europe are coming round to a more realistic appreciation of the situation. They realise that it is impossible for the debtor countries to fulfil their commitments on the original terms, and that a comprehensive repayment plan is essential, if worse problems are to be avoided. These include further worsening of world trade, since the reduction of imports forced on the debtor countries by the orthodox strategy would lead to a drop in the industrialised countries' exports. It should be remembered that 40 per cent of American exports go to the developing world; and that for the industrialised countries as a whole, this figure is 30 per cent.

Be that as it may, the insolvency of Argentina and the rescheduling of its foreign-debt payments is sure to create conflict with its creditors. It is clear that it must recover autonomy over its economic policy, and that the constitutional government cannot agree to become simply the administrator of the foreign debt on behalf of the IMF and the creditor banks. The situation is such that the Argentine authorities are not in a position to decide whether or not they can pay. Argentina should, however, avoid reneging on its debt and declaring a moratorium on payment. Whatever the causes of this debt were, they were legally binding contracts, and as such should be accepted as part of the nation's foreign liabilities. Argentina must avoid any such rash moves, since with the return of democracy it has recovered responsibility and prudence in the management of its foreign affairs.

The reasonableness of Argentina's position, and the vulnerability of the creditor banks to any declaration of bankruptcy on the part of its main debtors, will doubtless mean that no hasty action is taken. Sovereign loans (those contracted under independent national legal systems) may have great advantages but, at the same time, they cannot be reclaimed if the debtor is unable to fulfil his obligations.

Argentina should do everything possible to reach a negotiated solution that is compatible with an effective guarantee of its national sovereignty and the most pressing needs for the country's economic recovery. It is to be hoped that, in the end, an acceptable solution can be found. However, Argentines must be prepared for the worst. They should not think that the whole of the problem is the foreign debt, nor that everything will be solved once this is refinanced. Foreign debt or not, the country has to undertake a profound reform to rid its economic system of its fundamental imbalances and to free its possibilities for growth, whilst at the same time ensuring price stability and a balanced account in its international dealings. Argentina is emerging from a war and, like Europe in 1945, it has to be extremely strict regarding what is its scarcest resource: foreign currency. The fiscal and monetary reform which the present crisis demands also imposes a strict plan of priorities for imports and, of course, strict exchange rate control to avoid capital flight. The country must be ready *to live within its means* for as long as the present emergency lasts. This implies limiting the use of currency for essential imports of goods and services and for interest payments on the debt at the agreed time. Argentina is the only main debtor nation to be able to count on all the three following advantages: a surplus of foodstuffs, self-sufficiency in energy and a low mean rate of imports. It can, in effect, function and begin its revival with its own resources.

The renegotiation of the foreign debt forms part of a general situation whose importance far exceeds that of the relations between the Argentine government and the creditor banks. Argentina's international prestige is at stake. This makes it all the more essential to take the decision to resolve all the border disputes created by Argentina's unconstitutional governments peacefully and using diplomatic channels, and at the same time to reaffirm the validity of the freedom and dignity of the human being, values which are at the heart of Western civilisation and which have also been violated by its authoritarian governments. It is also necessary to widen the terms of debate about the foreign debt. The problem must be seen politically both within the country and internationally. Within the country, because the National Congress must give its full support, Argentina's future cannot be compromised solely by decisions taken by the Executive power. There must be a broad debate and a general consensus on the matter among the main political groupings in Argentina. Internationally, the renegotiation should include contacts and discussions with political, economic and financial sectors in the United States, Europe, and other centres of power. The negotiations should be led by representatives from the Argentine Congress as well as from the Executive if, as seems to me essential, the political terms of reference of this question are to be made as broad as possible.

Final success will depend on the results of the economic policy adopted by Argentina's constitutional government. If inflation can be controlled, economic performance improved, foreign payments met, and confidence in the country's future restored both at home and internationally, Argentina's bargaining position will be greatly strengthened. If, on the other hand, the government is unsuccessful in restoring economic order and getting the country moving again, there is little hope that the debt negotiations will be successful, and the risk of a clash with the international financial community will grow. This is why I am stressing that the task of restoring order within Argentina is paramount, and why I consider that the foreign debt is not, ultimately, the most important problem. It is rather a question which takes second place to that of creating a successful governmental system, one capable of breaking once and for all the vicious cycle of hyper-inflation combined with a contraction of the economy.

It is not the foreign creditors who will pose the greatest problem for the debt negotiations. They are after all just as keen as the Argentine government to avoid any break down, and to reach an acceptable solution. The greatest threat will come from those groups within our own country who have controlled affairs in recent years and who will do their utmost to destabilise the democratic government and prevent the success of a responsible policy based on the affirmation of sovereignty and economic growth. For these groups which still cling to the ideal of a pre-industrial Argentina, the middlemen for international credit and the wielders of authoritarian power, the orthodox strategy for debt payment and Argentina's international subordination are the only possible ways to consolidate their power, with or without the foreign debt, with or without the IMF. It is in this sense that the debt question takes on a political dimension which transcends its economic and financial aspects. No one should forget this.

Part II

The Social and Economic Pact: A Systematic Policy for the Constitutional Government

8

The choices facing Argentine society

The present crisis in the Argentine economy has worsened its problems of underdevelopment. The answers to the present problems will only be valid if they are part of a global policy aimed at overcoming the obstacles which, in the past, have prevented the formation of a modern industrial economy. The challenge facing the new constitutional regime goes beyond reducing inflation, improving the balance of payments, raising real wages and increasing output and employment. These challenges are in themselves daunting, but they offer no solution outside the framework of a viable policy of long-term growth.

The economic policy of the constitutional regime will have to tackle both the current crisis and the chronic aspects of underdevelopment. It is not enough to determine what monetary, fiscal and exchange policies are to be applied or to analyse the behaviour of the principal economic variables, the imbalances in the public sector, the balance of payments or relative prices. Essential as they are, these factors are not sufficient for a full understanding of the challenges Argentina faces. Inflation, unemployment and the balance-of-payments deficit cannot be eliminated without a radical change in Argentine development strategy, so it is essential to evaluate the basic conditions under which the long-term growth of the Argentine economy and its place in the international community should occur. A viable economic policy can emerge only from an analysis of the interaction between the current crisis and the historical process of underdevelopment. So, before considering the characteristics of the present crisis, we must consider the international context in which the new Argentine economic policy will be implemented and some important aspects of the Argentine situation, which will have a decisive influence on future events in the country. Let us start with the latter.

It will not be possible to impose the new economic policy arbitrarily. The monetarist policy imposed on 2 April 1976, could only be applied by means of the destruction of social pressure groups and savage repression. The constitutional regime's economic policy cannot be put into operation in this way, and the new policy must be based on the democratic principles of Argentine society. The historical background of the population, its tradition of social organisation and political development, have endowed it with a high level of information and the creation of strong organisations which represent the interests of workers and other social groups. Unlike some other developing countries, where cultural backwardness or the alienation from power of important sectors of the population results in a restricted participation in the democratic process, Argentina's democracy is characterised by a high level of participation. This was first seen in the period between the electoral reform of 1912 and the coming to power of the Radical Party in 1916, until the military coup of 1930. After World War II, and the electoral victory of the Peronist Party, popular participation increased and became more complex. These tendencies remained dormant under the unconstitutional governments which followed the 1955 coup and were repressed after the coup of 24 March 1976, but they survived and are now again a major influence in political behaviour.

These basic characteristics must be taken into account when economic policy is formulated. Also, in order to define economic policy one must assume that the new democratic regime will adopt certain basic criteria. There are two prerequisites for democracy and a successful economic policy. First, the new political administration must show restraint. That is to say, the distribution of power within the administration and also, in its negotiations with other social and economic sectors which, even if in the minority, still represent a substantial part of the process of capital accumulation and economic growth. Secondly, these minorities must accept the legitimate nature of the power held by the majority.

This is a major challenge which Argentine democracy has to face, and something which sets it apart from constitutional systems in other developing or industrialised countries. In many developing countries, the full participation of the majorities is restricted by a hegemony of elites which, even if guided by a spirit of change, maintain close links with the groups that hold economic power. Brazil and Mexico are two examples of this type of situation. In the industrialised countries, the high levels of development and welfare reached and the fact that economic power is held by national groups, mean that the Right has a wide political base and constitutes a viable electoral force. Argentina's situation is different. The conservative forces have not been a viable electoral alternative from the time of the 1912 electoral reform (when they lost the possibility of manipulating the electoral results) until 1930 with the military coup and the installation of fraud as a norm. They did not manage to increase their popular support or become a viable alternative in the democratic process during this period. This is because the strategy they proposed then, and have continued to propose ever since, is incompatible with industrialisation, integrated development, improved population distribution, independence from the international centres of power and more equal income distribution. The Right is ideologically tied to a pre-industrial model of the country and it is associated, by its economic and financial interests, to a primary-exporter economy. Its attempts at managing the economy — always under unconstitutional governments — have had serious consequences for industrial development, the economies of the regions and the welfare of the majority of the population. Its lack of popular support is therefore not surprising. One of the negative consequences of this political evolution is that the liberal principles of freedom, respect for human rights and for minority rights, which were the most valuable legacy from the conservative reformists of the latter part of the nineteenth century and the beginning of the twentieth century, were nullified by the orthodox economic policy and the attacks by unrepresentative minorities against the constitutional order.

Without popular support it is impossible to formulate consistent nationalist policies; nor is this possible with the populist abuse of power. The majority in Argentina seeks a change within the model of a mixed economy. The multiparty political opposition to the military government has repeatedly stated, from its first joint statement in December 1981, that it seeks to promote development, economic independence and social justice within a mixed economy, where the market will still be the main factor in determining resource allocation and income distribution. It was referring, however, to the national market, because it is clear that an under-industrialised country cannot absorb international price variations without hampering its possibilities of technical development and increasing the vulnerability of its productive system.

Profits and private investment must be crucial, if not exclusive, factors in determining economic growth. The private sector's expectations about growth, fiscal policy, external relations and price and income policies, have a decisive influence on economic performance. The question is whether an administration with popular support is compatible with a mixed economy and the process of transformation necessary to consolidate the productive structure, to create an integrated economy, to reduce inflation and to produce a sustained increase in the levels of participation and the standard of living. The answer is that Argentina *does* have the basic potential to embark on a joint effort of development and transformation, within the limits of a mixed economy.

The years 1946, 1958, 1963 and 1973 marked new starting points for Argentine democracy. On none of those occasions did it manage to become firmly established, and, from March 1976 to 1983, the country suffered the worst attacks ever on its national interests, welfare, freedom and human rights, at the hands of the military and the civilian elite. This massive attack on the fundamental values of our culture and our sovereignty culminated with war and defeat in the South Atlantic. The terrorist campaign which had threatened our internal security since the end of the 1960s was replaced by an uncontrolled abuse of power which oppressed most sectors of Argentine society.

The tragic experience of 1976 to 1983 and a history of more than fifty years of political instability and military coups, has left everyone in Argentina convinced that the country cannot continue to pay the high price of living outside the law. It cannot pay the economic cost, because the productive system has been pushed to the brink of collapse. Also, it cannot pay the price of putting at risk our sovereignty: in the Malvinas, where on 1 April 1982, there were only 1800 practically unarmed kelpers, there is now a powerful British garrison in the Argentine Sea which constitutes a serious threat to Argentina's territory and its rights in the South Atlantic and the Antarctic. Furthermore, the military regime re-opened the Beagle conflict and almost led the county into war with Chile. Argentina cannot afford further international discredit resulting from the violation of traditional Western values, as the West has always been its frame of reference both historically and politically.

This experience must have served as a lesson for the country about the consequences of military regimes and the attempts by the elites to take power. Furthermore, there has been an international reaction against the violation of basic values and the unpredictability of an unconstitutional regime which one day serves the interests of American policy in Central America and the next is at war with NATO. This has undermined support for those in Argentina who were the 'spoiled children' of the most reactionary sectors in the US and other international power centres.

All this leads us to believe that the story will not be repeated. Even those social and economic groups which in the past regarded the military governments as a viable alternative to the 'populist threat', have now learnt that an anti-national policy also affects their interests. That is to say that the new constitutional government can close the historical period which opened on 6 September 1930 and start a new one marked by democratic rule. The main reasons for this are:

1) The principal sectors of Argentine society have learnt from experience that it was division among them which prepared the ground for military coups and the disastrous rule by a minority. The experience of the multi-party opposition to the military regimes and the attitude adopted by the main political leaders indicate that this lesson has been learned. Naturally, the struggle for power and the normal dynamic of the democratic process will cause frictions and conflicts, but let us hope that these will never reach the stage of involving important sectors of public opinion in attempts to undermine institutional stability.

2) The economic evolution of the country until 1975 demonstrates the ineffectiveness of redistributive policies which are not based on the sustained growth of output and employment, on external equilibrium and on a reasonable stability of prices. The disaster caused by the monetarist experience begun on 2 April 1976, can be overcome with the adoption of an overall policy whose basic principles coincide with those included in the platforms of the major political groups. If such a policy were to be applied, Argentina's economic evolution would reinforce the bases for the development of a strong democracy.

3) There has been a split among the conservative forces between those groups whose long-term interests are in favour of the country's development and those which use financial speculation and bureaucratic power simply for their own ends. The former have an important role to play in the consolidation of the democratic process.

4) There is no room in the world today for an authoritarian and unpredictable Argentina. The current international situation acts to reinforce the democratic process in Argentina.

EFFECTS OF THE INTERNATIONAL CRISIS

Argentina's recent experience and the dominant tendencies in the world economy make a reappraisal of its development strategy and its international position a necessity.

The opening of the economy internationally through the application of an orthodox strategy failed in Argentina because it tried to establish a primary-exporter model and to prevent the formation of an integrated industrial system on a scale compatible with the size of the country. This opening also failed in countries like Brazil and Mexico, even though there it was restricted to the financial markets and did not affect traditional policies of industrialisation and import-substitution. These two countries grew rapidly throughout the 1970s but could not avoid the impact of the international financial crisis. At the beginning of the 1980s, they suffered serious imbalances and a reduction of output and employment. Like Argentina, but due to different mechanisms, they built up huge foreign debts and their economic policies became subordinated to the dictates of transnational capital. Throughout Latin America, countries face the challenge of rethinking their development strategies and their international position, as they did in the 1930s. The world's centres of power have changed the rules of the game, and the economies of the Latin American countries have been forced to adjust. Monetarism could only be applied in Argentina after 1976 because there was an unconditional supply of international credit, and because, until the second oil crisis of 1979–80, interest rates were low and international trade and the prices of primary products were quite favourable. However, the change in American monetary policy (towards the end of the Carter Administration), widespread protectionist practices in the industrialised countries, increased subsidies to exports of grains and other agricultural products in the US and the EEC, and the deterioration of the terms of trade for food and other primary products (including oil since 1982), have radically altered the conditions under which the opening to transnational capital and the increased indebtedness of the Latin American countries occurred. This sudden change of the rules of the game and the conditions prevailing in the world markets caused a crisis of confidence and showed that the debtors could not honour their commitments on the agreed terms. The rapid reduction of credit flows to Latin America then served to deepen the crisis.

There are no prospects of a substantial recovery of the world economy in the short or medium term. The industrialised countries are still caught in their own dilemmas. Both Keynesian and orthodox policies have proved incapable of guaranteeing full employment with reasonable price stability, and sustained expansion of trade and other international transactions. The conclusions to be drawn from the present world situation, and in particular that of Latin America and Argentina, are clear and can be summarised as follows:

1) *Development strategy:* The domestic market, industrialisation, the integration of the different manufacturing sectors and regional development policies have again become crucial elements in the growth process. The circumstances under which the re-emergence of the domestic dimension of the development process has occurred are very different now from those prevailing in the 1930s, when world recession also disrupted international trade relations. In spite of the monetarist disaster, Argentina has an important domestic market, diversified resources (including food and energy), a reasonable average income and savings potential and, above all, valuable human resources with a high cultural and technical level. Furthermore, technological change is increasing the possibilities of domestic industrial development. According to Jorge Sabato, 'economies of scale' are being replaced by 'economies to scale'; that is to say, the modern technology is being adapted to the plant size and resource availability of each country. Argentina has within its borders all the crucial elements for development: a domestic market, natural resources, human capital and savings potential. The answer to the world crisis and the internal problems must be found within Argentina. This also applies for all the other major countries in Latin America.

2) *Opening the economy:* In the current situation, it is impossible to isolate our economy from the rest of the

world. Even if natural resources and industrial activity
were diversified enough to allow a low level of imports,
international links would be crucial for technological
development and to widen potential supply and demand.
The rejection of the monetarist opening of the economy and
the transnationalisation of the economic system is not
based on an isolationist position, but on a disagreement
with the deeper implications of that type of approach. No
underdeveloped country has ever managed to progress
through the early transnationalisation of its productive
system and, even less, through the subordination of its
economic policy to the dominant interests of the international market. The US in the last century, Japan after the Meiji
restoration and particularly since 1945, Korea in the last
two decades; all these are countries which, with different
strategies, grew very rapidly. All of them had control over
the allocation of resources, rejected flexible exchange rates,
and manipulated policy instruments to achieve their
national objectives. It is not a matter of cutting Argentina
off from the international economy, but of opening the
economy in a controlled manner, based on an integration
of the internal market and on industrialisation. This means
ending the dependence on static comparative advantages
generated by underdevelopment and the creation of dynamic new comparative advantages based on technological
change and the increasing incorporation of added value to
primary production. The transnationalisation imposed by
the foreign power centres and by those internal groups
which subordinate national objectives to their interests is
incompatible with economic development, welfare, price
stability and balanced foreign payments. Argentina's experience over the last seven years clearly shows that the
model of transnational dependence can only bring about
the destruction of wealth, combined with soaring inflation
and foreign indebtedness. The constitutional government
has to face the difficult challenge presented by the world
order and the need to establish Argentina's economy
internationally.

3) *Resources:* It will be difficult for Argentina, given its

current foreign debt, to find external credit to cover the deficit on the balance-of-payments current account, before it can meet its debt interest payments. Even if the principal and all, or most, of the interest that is now due were to be refinanced, the international banking system is tending to reduce credit flows to the developing world and particularly to Argentina and the rest of Latin America. A firm investment policy, the recovery of international prestige and a change of expectations will probably generate credit flows from suppliers and direct private investment. However, this will only be possible if the government manages to mobilise spare capacity, to control inflation and to formulate a viable strategy to deal with the foreign debt.

Orthodox economists claim that the only way to mobilise resources to stimulate the productive system is to attract foreign credit or encourage the return of domestic capital which has left the country. They argue that the only alternative would be to print more money, and this would only raise inflation without increasing output. This argument is, of course, false, because there is no way in which the debt can be increased or capital repatriated without a change in expectations. The effect that domestic credit will have on the price level, within a programme of economic recovery, will depend on the consistency of the comprehensive economic policy to mobilise spare capacity and to increase output and real income. The orthodox argument that the effect of an increase in the money supply will be different according to whether it is generated by domestic credit or by an increase of international reserves through foreign credit or the repatriation of capital is inconsistent. In both cases, liquidity would increase and a divergence would arise between the expectations of the economic operators and the ability of the authorities to maintain their exchange policy. In terms of the effects on money supply, it does not matter whether the growth in the monetary base is caused by an increase of the internal or the external assets of the Central Bank.

The necessary resources are to be found in the national economy. They stem from the large amount of spare capacity and the high levels of unemployment and under-employment. The constitutional government has to use that potential. It will be shown later that fiscal and monetary policies and a social pact can offer viable solutions to the problem. The increase in output and income will generate the necessary resources to improve real wages and, at the same time, raise the levels of savings and capital formation. When the country reaches full employment, the problem will have to be dealt with differently.

Until the crisis is overcome, the country must understand that it has to pay its own way, that is to say, to manage with its own resources and the foreign-payments capacity generated by exports. It will only be able to achieve this by means of a strict policy of selective imports, the reconstruction of its industrial capacity, and the expansion of exports. Domestic savings and the capacity to earn foreign currency are the only available solutions for facing the crisis and to put the country to work. These resources exist within the country and there is no possibility of solving the problems of the Argentine economy from the outside.

4) *Social implications:* The monetarist model collapsed because of its economic effects and because it impoverished the majority of the Argentine people. Argentina suffered even more than Brazil and Mexico where, even if there were no solutions to the problems of extreme poverty, there was at least a substantial increase in employment. The international crisis brought out into the open a situation which could not be sustained for much longer in Argentina and the rest of Latin America. As in the 1930s, the world crisis increased the tensions which had been building up in the country and which showed the ineffectiveness of the prevailing development models. Exactly the same is happening now. Whether the process of transnationalisation is 'Argentine style' or 'Brazilian style', poverty is unacceptable in countries whose econmic potential is capable of satisfying the most pressing social needs. That is why any strategy to solve the crisis must take into account the social dimension. The improvement of real wages, the formulation of programmes to eradicate extreme poverty and

marginalisation, and the creation of new mechanisms of negotiation among the different sectors of society, are all essential elements of any policy to build democracy in Argentina. This social dimension is the obverse of a development strategy oriented towards the internal market and the process of industrialisation. The improvement of overall purchasing power is crucial to widen the internal market and to create incentives for private investment.

9

The situation in 1984

The constitutional government of Argentina has inherited the worst economic crisis in the country's history. The new authorities have found themselves with a massive deterioration of the productive system and a huge foreign debt, together with serious distortions in relative prices and an enormous budget deficit. The economic situation at the time when the new authorities took over is summarised in the following sections.

The dominant feature was the low level of industrial output. In 1983, manufacturing output was similar to that in 1970 and 20 per cent less than in 1974. If we consider that industrial output had been growing at an annual rate of 6 per cent until the middle of the 1970s, we can conclude that manufacturing output in 1983 was 50 per cent lower than it would have been if the same growth rate had been maintained. The industrial recession hit the wage-goods areas particularly hard as well as those areas subject to international competition. In the first case, because income in the wage-earning sector had declined by 40 per cent (because of a fall in real wages and a reduction in employment), there was a much lower demand for durable goods, textiles and shoes. In the second case, it was because of a massive inflow of imports, following the devaluation of the peso and a reduction in tariffs, which provided substitutes for local production. This also had serious effects in the two most important sectors of modern industry: capital goods and electronics. The textile industry suffered from the combined effects of a fall in income and competition from imports. This explains why the volume of textile production declined by more than 40 per cent between 1974 and 1983. For the same reason, the production of shoes fell by 60 per cent. Recently, there has been a moderate improvement in some of these areas as a result of the devaluation of the peso and a decline in imports. However, this recovery is limited by levels of demand which are substantially lower than those prevailing in the middle of the 1970s. There was no sharp fall in the demand for food, because of its income inelasticity. The capital goods industries were affected by the reduction in capital formation (in 1982 investment in durable equipment was 35 per cent less than in 1974) and the substitution of nationally produced machinery by imports.

What is the current level of spare capacity? An average of 40 per cent to 50 per cent of total capacity; that is to say, the same proportion of actual to potential manufacturing output. However, it should be remembered that in times of full employment, the level of spare capacity is still approximately 20 per cent. This means that about 30 per cent of spare capacity could be used without requiring fresh capital investment. The question is whether this 30 per cent includes plant which is unusable because of closures, obsolescence, the dismantling of equipment, or reductions in size of the firms that are still operating. This question cannot at present be adequately answered because of insufficient information.

The economies of Argentina's regions and the construction industry were also seriously affected by monetarist policies. The pace at which these sectors recover under the new economic policy will indicate whether or not there is spare capacity and the possibility of expanding supply in the short term without further fixed capital investment.

The agricultural sector of the *pampas* (wet grasslands) grew, from 1976 on, at the same rate that it had during the two previous decades, although there was probably a slowing down of the rate of technical innovation and investment which had produced a progressive recovery since the beginning of the 1950s. On the other hand, between 1974 and 1983, the cattle stock fell by approximately 10 million head. This is the result of the negative effects of monetarist policy on the real income of this sector, the international market situation and the worsening of relative prices of meat as against cereals. The absence of a consistent policy to expand the cattle zone in compensation for the displacement of cattle from traditional areas, resulted in an insufficient supply for the demands of the internal and export markets. Domestic consumption is currently approximately 65 kg per year per person and exports (meat and bone) are about 400,000 tons per year; these are the lowest levels of recent times.

There should be no short-term shortages in the infra-structure sectors (excluding oil) following high levels of investment, before and after 1976, on energy, transport and communications. Oil production, on the other hand, has remained stagnant. This could lead to supply shortages for the internal market and the need to increase imports, which would be financially impossible given the present balance-of-payments situation.

WAGES AND EMPLOYMENT

Real wages bore the brunt of the decline in output and income. Between 1974 and 1983, output per capita fell by 20 per cent and potential output by 50 per cent. This dramatic fall in average income and welfare (in relation to expectations created by previous growth rates), was absorbed by a decline in the standard of living of the working class. Real wages fell more than average income, which means that there was a transfer of income from the wage-earning sector to the rest of society. The share of wages in national income fell from 50 per cent in 1974 to 35 per cent in 1983. This is partly explained by a transfer of wage-earners to self-employment. According to household surveys, between 1974 and 1982 self-employment increased from 18 per cent to 22 per cent of the total working population. However, this only explains 15 per cent of the reduction of the share of wages in national income. Most of it is due to transfers of income to other sectors.

The labour market changed substantially between 1976

and 1983. Apart from the increase in self-employment, there was a rapid increase in the number of pensioners. Industrial employment fell sharply. Until 1974, it had been growing at an annual rate of 1.3 per cent. Between 1974 and 1983, the number of workers fell from 1.6 million to 1.3 million, approximately the same as the number registered at the beginning of the 1950s. The supply of marginal labour (women, adolescents and older people) diminished with the fall in real wages, since they became insufficient to offset the costs of travelling to work and of seeking employment. The same occurred with migrant labour from Paraguay, Bolivia and Chile. The fall in real wages reduced the supply of this labour, particularly in the construction industry. Argentine workers, mainly skilled, also emigrated. In the absence of updated statistics on migration it is difficult to quantify this movement of labour, but the numbers involved must have been very high. All these developments have important repercussions. First, it means that the official unemployment rate underestimates the real one. Even so, the official rate doubled between 1975 and 1983 (2.4 per cent and 4.7 per cent respectively in March), after having reached a low of 1.8 per cent in 1980, when self-employment was at its peak. Secondly, observable under-employment increased (from 6·2 per cent to 7·8 per cent between 1975 and 1982). Disguised under-employment also increased (low productivity occupations). Finally, it means that when the economic recovery eventually takes place, it will be more difficult to attract labour away from self-employment and under-employment, particularly in the case of skilled labour which has switched to self-employment.

It is interesting to note that while employment fell by 40 per cent between 1974 and 1983, industrial output fell by only 20 per cent. This means that labour productivity increased by 3 per cent annually. This uncharacteristic form of productivity growth replaced that which had prevailed in the middle 1970s, when employment and global output were increasing. At that time, the annual rate of increase of productivity in manufacturing industry was 5 per cent.

THE PUBLIC SECTOR

The economic recession and the deficit generated by the collapse of firms and financial institutions (a deficit absorbed by the Central Bank through an expansion of the money supply), produced a dramatic increase in the public sector's share of the national economy. It was approximately 20 per cent of GNP throughout the 1976–83 period. Employment in the public sector for that period was approximately 1.8 million, that is to say, about 20 per cent of the work-force. The fall in real wages in the public sector tended to reduce this sector's share of national income, without substantially modifying the levels prevailing in the middle of the previous decade.

On the other hand, the government's use of resources increased sharply. Public expenditure on administration (central, provincial and municipal), plus investment on state-owned enterprises, increased from 30 per cent of GDP at the beginning of the 1970s to 40 per cent in 1983. Similarly, taxes (including contributions to the social welfare system), increased from 20 per cent at the beginning of the 1970s to 26 per cent in 1980. This increase in the relative weight of public expenditure and of taxes was not the result of an increase in the rate of growth of economic activity in this sector, as compared to the previous decade. What happened was that the rest of the economy was stagnant. Military expenditure did increase, but there is no accurate information about this area. The deficit created by the collapse of financial institutions after the April 1980 crisis, which was financed by the Central Bank by means of an expansion of the monetary system, must also be taken into account, as it represented 40 per cent of the growth of the monetary base for the period 1980–83.

There has been a switch of public expenditure away from basic social services, such as health and education, in favour of military and security expenditure. There are no reliable data on security expenditure, because it spreads across different areas of the budget, or on imports of military equipment after the 1976 coup. However, the information that is available indicates that expenditure in these two areas, which in the middle of the last decade was 2 per cent of GNP, has increased substantially.

INFLATION

At the beginning of 1984, the rate of inflation was about 300 per cent, approximately ten times higher than the average for the 1945–75 period. In such a situation, economic decisions are distorted by the need to protect the value of stocks, financial assets and income from the effects of inflation. Any errors of judgment as to the effects of inflation can have disastrous consequences for the firms involved and their employees. All this, added to a lack of stability of relative prices creates a climate of confusion which inhibits investment, the adoption of measures to improve productivity and medium- and long-term financial planning.

A reasonable balance in relative prices is crucial for the constitutional government. Otherwise, the government will have to adopt drastic measures to update, for example, public service charges and the rate of exchange, and this will only produce sudden redistributions of income, that can only add to the present tension and confusion. In this respect, real wages, which have fallen further below their historical average than any other category, will have to be raised in a way that is compatible with a fair distribution of income and an increase in output and employment.

EXPECTATIONS

Recent experience has created a climate of negative expectations which affects all the economic and social sectors. There is a general feeling that 'tomorrow can only be worse than today'. This situation hinders any possibility of economic recovery which, ultimately, depends on a change of attitudes. The damage caused by the military government goes beyond the creation of poverty and a huge debt. It also led the country to defeat and betrayed the fundamental values of our society. The climate of pessimism as the constitutional government took power was not restricted to the economic area.

10

An economic strategy for the constitutional government

BOOSTING THE ECONOMY, DEALING WITH THE FOREIGN DEBT AND
AN ANTI-INFLATIONARY PROGRAMME

The constitutional government should make raising the level of welfare a priority. The fall in real wages, unemployment, the isolation and worsening of social conditions in the interior, has created tensions that will break out into the open now democratic rule has been re-established. The most crucial and urgent objective should be to raise the standard of living and to eliminate extreme poverty, which affects large sectors of the population.

In order to raise the standard of living, it is necessary to increase the production of goods and services and to aim at a more equal distribution of income. This involves mobilising spare capacity and unemployed and under-employed labour. The Argentine economy is functioning below its productive potential and it should be possible to achieve an immediate recovery of output and real income with the existing capital stock, if inflation is brought under control and a deficit on the balance-of-payments current account is avoided.

So, the problem the new government has to solve is: how to boost the economy, while keeping down inflation and meeting its international payment commitments. To answer this, four major areas have to be taken into account: demand management, income redistribution and resource allocation, balance of payments, and prices. Let us examine each of these points in turn.

1) *Demand management:* Given the current public deficit, the recovery of demand will depend on private expenditure and international trade. The first category consists of private consumption and investment. The largest share of private

consumption corresponds to the wage-earners. So, in order to increase private consumption, it is essential to raise real wages. Private investment is dependent on the level of spare capacity, interest rates, the rate of growth of the economy and entrepreneurial expectations. These expectations will probably be raised when the national economy recovers and the institutional situation has stabilised. Furthermore, the promotion, from the beginning of the process of recovery, of large investment projects in basic industries, housing and other sectors, would accelerate the participation of private investment in the expansion of aggregate demand.

Initially, the increase in internal industrial output will produce a rise in imports, which will, however, be limited by the level of exports and the restrictions imposed by the foreign debt. A firm imports policy will be required to limit the demand for foreign currency and to direct consumption towards the internal market. Exports will grow if there is a consistent policy of incentives and a sensible exchange rate. The net effect of international trade, assuming that a modest surplus were used to pay some of the interest on the debt, will be neutral. The most important impact of foreign trade will be on productivity, because imported inputs will diversify the supply of consumption and capital goods and the promotion of exports will develop areas of specialisation and increase the scale of production.

The public sector will also play an important part in raising the level of aggregate demand, not by increasing the budget deficit, but by changing the tax structure and the composition of public expenditure, which will have a crucial impact on income distribution, resource allocation and economic growth.

2) *Income distribution and resource allocation:* The initial increase in real wages and industrial incentives required to boost consumption and private investment will be financed in the long term from the income generated by the use of existing spare capacity. In the short term, however, it must be financed by a reduction in the unit costs of production. Real borrowing rates and the costs of financial intermedia-

tion must be reduced to the minimum compatible with a viable monetary programme and the existence of an efficient and competitive financial system.

The State is a major consumer of goods and services; it can influence income distribution through public expenditure, taxation and policies to finance the budget deficit. This deficit should be progressively reduced and the relation of taxation and of public expenditure to GDP should not exceed 24 per cent and 38 per cent, respectively, to achieve the neutral effect on aggregate demand described in the previous section. The state will still play a crucial role in the phase of recovery, by reorganising public expenditure, allocating resources and returning to the private sector the firms that came under official control as a result of the crisis created by the monetarist policy.

Relative prices of primary and industrial production and of goods and services are also crucial in determining income distribution and resource allocation. The relative prices of products subject to international competition (exports and import substitutes) improved considerably, following a series of massive devaluations which started at the beginning of 1981. This was particularly noticeable in the case of agricultural production from the rich region of the *pampas*. Also, real income in this sector increased as a result of good harvests in the period 1982–3 and a recovery of real prices for cattle. An increase in real wages and private investment in manufacturing industry depends on the future stability of real prices for primary production which will guarantee adequate levels of return for the agricultural industry. The new administration will also have to ensure that, with the recovery of aggregate demand, there is no deterioration in the relative prices of goods against services.

Finally, resource allocation between consumption and investment re-emerges as a crucial element in determining the level of utilisation of the productive system and its long-term growth. The immediate recovery of real wages and incentives for private investment will evolve, as explained above, from a policy of income redistribution. Once the economy is working at a satisfactory level of utilisation of its potential capacity, further improvements in the standard of living and economic growth will depend on the consistency of the relation between wages and productivity, taxes and disposable income, interest rate and private return on investment, and effective exchange rates and domestic prices. Ultimately, capital formation will depend on private savings and investment and on the volume and multiplier effect of public investment. Technological change and reallocation of resources towards the growth sectors are instrumental in improving productivity. However, savings and capital formation are still essential requisites for development.

3) *Balance of payments:* If the policy regarding international payments becomes subordinated to the repayment of the foreign debt, it will be impossible to formulate any global policy for recovery and economic growth. The possibility of importing will be limited by the earnings derived from exports. Flows of international credit will probably begin again when the Argentine economy starts to recover. In the short term, however, the growth in output and real income will depend on the growth rate of exports. It is unlikely that the income elasticity of imports can be reduced to less than 1:3. Even though Argentina is very rich in resources, including food and energy, and has one of the lowest import coefficients in the world (less than 10 per cent), a recovery of the national economy would inevitably increase the demand for imported inputs. Imports will tend to grow at a faster rate than economic activity. To compensate for this, exports ought to grow at a rate at least 30 per cent higher than the rate of growth of GDP. In other words, if the country cannot overcome the problems of insufficient exports and recurrent balance-of-payments crises, it will be impossible to sustain a long-term growth of output and real income.

4) *Prices:* The economy cannot function with the present rates of inflation. If this problem is not solved, the country will be trapped forever between the frustration of military governments and the failure of democracy. There are basically two anti-inflationary strategies: the orthodox one

and that based on a widespread political agreement. The first consists of reducing liquidity until unemployment and spare capacity discourage any claims for higher wages or prices. This strategy requires a drastic reduction in public expenditure and a balanced budget. The cuts in public expenditure must be very large to compensate for the reduction of tax revenue that would result from the fall in real income. This strategy has proved ineffective, even under dictatorial regimes, because it carries with it enormous social costs, the destruction of wealth, the reduction of the national economy to the role of exporter of food and primary products, and the elimination of the State as an instrument for the development of Argentine society.

By definition, the orthodox strategy is incompatible with the existence of legitimate power and democracy. The only viable policy to control inflation is one of economic reorganisation and political agreement to determine income distribution and relative prices.

THE AUTONOMY OF ECONOMIC POLICY

We have explained how the monetarist policy of the military regimes tried to subordinate Argentina's economy to the international centres of power, with the full cooperation of an internal elite whose interests correspond to the primary-exporter model. In this context, the State could no longer act as the promoter of development and economic independence, but was relegated to the role of administrator of the foreign debt.

It would be a mistake to consider the foreign debt exclusively as an economic problem. It is basically a political problem, because it determines the evolution of the Argentine economy and the distribution of power. The political dimension of the foreign debt has two aspects. Internationally, it reflects the conflict between the centres of power and the developing countries; that is to say, the North–South debate. Internally, it reflects the confrontation between those who benefit from a dependent and anti-democratic country and the majority, which is fighting for development and democracy.

The constitutional government will never succeed unless it considers the foreign-debt problem in these terms. It must decide to recover the independence of the national economy, by formulating a realistic policy to deal with the debt. This does not mean that the government should refuse to honour the debt created by the monetarists and the aggressive policy of penetration by the international banking system, but that it does not have to accept their terms unconditionally. These terms will have to be reconsidered. The United States and the rest of the industrialised countries also have their problems and will have to negotiate.

The early international opening of an underdeveloped dependent economy hinders any possibility for national development. This was the long-term objective of the monetarist policy. The problem is not new: it is a historical conflict that Argentina has not yet resolved and that reappears now in the context of an extremely complex international and domestic situation.

THE ECONOMIC AND SOCIAL PACT

The economic situation inherited by the constitutional government is unprecedented in Argentine, or indeed world history. The current combination of high inflation, low real wages, a large idle spare capacity, and a huge foreign-payments deficit is completely atypical. Usually, inflation and foreign deficits occur at the end of a period of expansion, when full utilisation of available capacity and the labour force lead to a push for salary increases, a reduction in goods available for export, and a rise in imports. When there is high unemployment and spare capacity, Argentina normally experiences price stability and a surplus in its international payments. These *normal* situations will arouse expectations which are very different from those to be found at present among companies and the work-force in Argentina. With high rates of inflation, high wages, and a foreign deficit, economic agents would expect measures to curb demand, contain salaries and profits, and to meet the foreign payments. On the other hand, if there is a recession, they would expect policies to stimulate demand in order to raise production and real wages.

But in the current situation in Argentina, these expectations are also *abnormal*. With high inflation rates and a large external deficit, the labour force is demanding increases in real wages and firms are trying to restore their profit levels. Such a situation cannot be left to the free play of market forces. If the Argentine financial market were to continue linked to the international one, and the present free exchange policy pursued, the interest rate and the size of the surplus which would be needed in the balance-of-payments current account would only depress still further production, employment, and real wages. It would therefore become necessary to apply drastic measures to reduce public expenditure and liquidity. However, even if the Argentine financial market were to be isolated from the international one by enforcing strict exchange controls and keeping the peso well-undervalued, the traditional instruments of economic policy would not be able to resolve the present abnormal situation.

If, for example, the government tried to boost demand by increasing public expenditure and the budget deficit and, in addition, increasing credit flows to the private sector and lowering the rate of interest set by the Central Bank, firms and workers would expect higher inflation. To service the debt, the rate of exchange would have to be in line with the rate of inflation, and so the foreign payments would add to the process of inflation. Under such conditions, it would be impossible to expand the economy; that is, to boost demand and real wages to stimulate an increase in the supply of goods and services. In such a context, the speculative pressure against the peso would be unmanageable, the gap between the official and the black market rate of exchange would stimulate capital flight, and the real interest rate could fall to such low levels that it would reduce liquidity in the system to the minimum compatible with the demand for money for transactions.

Thus, neither free market forces nor the traditional instruments of economic policy can work in the present situation. This is the result of a profound crisis and, therefore, it calls for a political solution, which can only work within the context of the type of economic policy described.

It is essential to establish a social pact which would condition the expectations and claims of the different sectors. It is also necessary to create a united internal front to formulate policies to deal with the foreign debt without hindering the possibilities of economic recovery. Argentina will only be able to negotiate with the IMF and the international banks on terms that are compatible with its national interest if it has a realistic programme of internal adjustment and economic recovery. A social pact is also required not merely to deal with the most pressing issues such as inflation and the debt, but also to decide on the country's long-term objectives.

It is interesting that this emergence of a social pact as a crucial element of economic policy in Argentina, coincides with similar trends in the rest of the world. The Labour Government in Australia is relying on an economic and social pact. Even in the US and Western Europe, there is a growing demand for this type of approach as an alternative to orthodox policies, which only create unemployment and recession, and Keynesian policies which are no longer able to guarantee full employment with reasonable price stability. The new approach would have an internal dimension of agreement between entrepreneurs and workers, and an international dimension of coordination among the industrialised countries, whose interdependence severely limits the degree of autonomy of their own national policies.

The need for a Social and Economic Pact is even more urgent in Argentina since it not only has to recover from a grave economic crisis but also has to reconstruct its democratic system. The Pact cannot be limited to an agreement on prices and wages, but should extend over wider areas of the economy. Also, it should be part of a consistent overall strategy, in which the State undertakes certain commitments as to the management of crucial economic variables such as the interest rate and the exchange rate. The Pact should therefore involve the entrepreneurs, the workers and the public sector and should cover, in addition to agreements on prices and wages, the following areas:

• *Public sector:* the structure and level of taxation and of public expenditure, the budget deficit and the prices of public services;

• *Monetary policy:* real interest rates and reform of the financial system to reduce its costs and to transform it into an efficient instrument of resource allocation;

• *Balance of payments:* effective exchange rates, refunds and deductions and criteria for the negotiation of the foreign debt; and,

• *Economic expansion:* public investment programmes and incentives for private investment to boost demand and to increase productive capacity, regional programmes and special programmes for specific industries, housing programmes and social infrastructure.

The public must be kept informed of all the stages of the formulation and application of the Pact. Success and sustained participation by all social sectors will only be achieved when the secrecy imposed on economic and foreign policy by the previous military governments is ended. The democratic authorities must provide information on all the main issues, such as the size and composition of the budget. Expenditure on security and defence must be approved by Congress, as in all democratic societies. Internal security and national defence must be considered part of the overall objectives established by Argentine society through its legitimate representatives.

The guidelines of the Pact would be worked out by the Executive and presented to Congress for approval. Then the Executive Power would establish means of consultation with representative organisations from the different social sectors. They would study the contents of the Pact and its repercussion on their sectorial interests.

Congress could create a special commission to ensure that everyone complies with the terms of the agreement. The Planning Department of the Ministry of Economics would handle the claims put forward by the different sectors regarding the enforcement of the Economic and Social Pact. The application of the Pact would require the active participation of the provincial governments, and the Federal Investment Council could be the technical body to coordinate the different areas of the Pact.

The central government would provide up-to-date information on the performance of the economy and on the application of its policies, in order to allow for any necessary adjustments. The Pact should not be rigid concerning income distribution and resource allocation that might hinder technological change, capital accumulation and the strengthening of Argentina's international position.

In the long term, the Pact will probably become the habitual mechanism for the formulation and enforcement of economic and social policies. In the present Argentine situation, however, it would be better if it were established in the first place for a definite length of time; no more than that necessary for the resolution of the crisis and the laying of bases for a strong, viable economy. The Pact would then be seen in the context of a national emergency, and the government would have the necessary support to impose the harsh policies required if the crisis inherited from the monetarist disaster and the dictatorial regimes is to be overcome.

11

The commitments of the
Social and Economic Pact

INCREASING THE REAL WAGE. HOW TO FINANCE IT.

An improvement in the workers' purchasing power must
be achieved by implementing a wage increase as soon as
the Pact is created. The size of this wage settlement will be
determined by the level of real wages at the time when the
new economic policy is put into practice and the state of the
different variables in the economic system. The limits to this
initial increase in salaries will be the following:

1) *An increase in the participation of wage-earners in national
income without the creation of inflationary pressures:* The
effect of the increase in salaries on production costs,
averaged throughout the economy, corresponds to the
participation of wage earners in national income.

This share, currently at 35 per cent, is well below its
historical average, for example, 45 per cent in the 1960–75
period. It cannot be improved in the short term without
producing uncontrollable inflationary pressures. The
answer is to create an increase in real income. This would
allow an improvement in real wages and a greater increase
of the wage earners' share without reducing the absolute
income levels of other social sectors. However, in the
context of a revival of the economy and better production
and real income, the economic system will be able to
accommodate an income redistribution at the beginning
which favours the wage-earners. The terms of the Pact will
set the limits of this redistribution. It will mean a drop in the
profit margins on company sales, which can be compatible
with an increase in the profitability of capital invested, as
long as there is an increase in the volume of production.

2) *A simultaneous reduction of other costs:* It is the financial

and fixed costs which will have to be lowered in order to accommodate an increase in the price of labour per unit of production. The first of these can be achieved by lowering the real interest rates. In addition, as part of the monetary plan, special lines of credit could be extended in order to pay for the increase in working capital caused by higher wages. A reduction in fixed costs depends on increasing sales and the volume of production. There is, therefore, a circular causal link between the initial increase in salaries and consumer demand, boosting sales and the reduction of fixed costs. In this way, the increase in salaries should pay for itself.

The government's wage policy should pay particular attention to the progress of basic wage settlements. There are two reasons for this: first, in order to restore the purchasing power of the lowest strata; and, secondly, so that the wages policy and the collective wage agreements can truly act to guide the evolution of real incomes.

Wage levels and their increase in the first stages of the new economic policy must be established in the Economic and Social Pact. Collective labour agreements can be entered into once this first phase has been accomplished; a phase in which, it is to be hoped, the inflation rate will have been substantially reduced and the economy will have begun its recovery. If the wage settlements are to be granted from the very beginning of the new economic plan, they must be in line with the provisions of the Economic and Social Pact.

An increase in the minimum wage is also an absolute necessity. The real minimum wage has fallen by 25 per cent since 1975. A restoration of this minimum wage is essential to satisfy the most pressing demands of the lowest-paid groups. At present, the minimum wage is sufficient only for 25 per cent of a normal household's basic needs. The government's wage policy must aim to improve this situation.

After the initial increase in salaries, they must then be adjusted to fit in with the overall strategy aimed at stabilising the economy. Any further increases must be linked to an increase in the productivity of those companies directly involved in the revival of the economy. Taking the economy as a whole, if we suppose that each person's income is to increase by 15 per cent between 1984 and 1986, one could expect an increase in real wages of 30 per cent over the same period.

The recovery in the workers' standard of living is not based solely on these increases in real wages. Average salaries will also improve as a result of the transfer of labour from marginal, un-productive activities with low wages, to the industrial and other sectors with a higher average wage per employee. An increase in employment will also push up the aggregate of wages and family income. Better health, education and social services will lead to an improvement in welfare that is not directly reflected in higher real wages.

As far as the non-active population goes, an expansion of employment will permit a slowdown in the rapid growth of the numbers of retired people (which grew at an annual rate of 5.6 per cent between 1975 and 1982), and will improve the financial position of the benefit system. There must be a greater increase in the pensions of the lowest-paid, and in those of the oldest citizens, and the special pension categories must be revised.

PRICES

Once the guidelines of the wages policy have been laid down, a drastic reduction in inflation levels would be based on the following main strategies:

1) *A fixed lending rate and fixed spread for financial dealings:* the monetary authority must fix a nominal lending rate, together with the spread, to take into account the drastic reduction in the rate of inflation. This is essential if inflation is to be curbed, and in turn can only be maintained if the inflation rate is cut. This policy will only be effective if the real lending rate, the sum of the nominal rate set by the monetary authority plus the effective increase in prices, can be kept within annual limits of between zero and 5 per cent. This must be achieved if the monetary reform programme is to be effective and a satisfactory balance of payments

created. A strongly negative interest rate would depress money demand and curb the expansion of credit. It would, at the same time, put further speculative pressure on the peso and widen the gap between official and unofficial exchange rates. However, any overall economic programme which aims at internal consistency must include a stabilisation policy that starts with the introduction of an interest rate considerably lower than the current one.

2) *Charges for public services* (*energy, communications, transport*): these represent costs for companies and expenditure for consumers. As with the interest rate, a policy for stabilising the economy must start with a monthly rate of increase in these charges that is substantially lower than is currently the case. Once again, such a policy will only be feasible if the inflation rate is effectively reduced. If this were not done, the worsening in real terms of the state-run firms' income would cause an impossibly large imbalance in the fiscal accounts and an expansion in public sector credit incompatible with the monetary programme as envisaged within the general economic stabilisation programme. Any such policy for services should include private transport.

3) *Exchange rates*: Given the current balance-of-payments situation and starting from a viable exchange rate, the rate should be kept at a level which accurately reflects the increase in domestic costs minus international inflation rates.

Consequently, the public sector would take the lead in the stabilisation policy by committing itself to regulating the variables which are to a large extent under its control: interest rates, charges for public services, and the exchange rate. If these were set at, say, a monthly rate of 3 or 4 per cent, one might well ask, why not less, so that their anti-inflationary impact could be still greater? The answer is that the rhythm of inflation will continue at a relatively high level despite success with the policy, because of the impossibility of an immediate reduction of more than a limited part of the fiscal deficit and its effect on the monetary system, and also because a number of readjustments of relative prices will be necessary. Once the deficit is under control and the changes in relative prices have been carried out, the stabilising strategy for the economy should aim for a second round of reductions in the rate of price increases, using the same mechanisms as were used during the first stages of the Pact.

This stabilising strategy, which relies on the government taking effective action to influence those variables over which it has control, will only truly work if two further conditions are fulfilled. First it will be necessary for all the fiscal, monetary and balance-of-payments policies to be coherent. Second, there will need to be a sharp slowdown in the price rises for goods and services produced by the private sector.

The first of these two points is dealt with in greater detail later in this book, since it is a central concern of the Economic and Social Pact. It is enough to indicate here that a slowdown in inflation depends on containing the fiscal deficit within limits imposed by: the necessary expansion of private credit, a real increase in the offer of goods and services, the behaviour of the demand for domestic credit by the public, and a stabilising of the current account on the balance of payments (once an agreement has been reached about the possibilities of paying the interest due on the foreign debt). If consistency in these areas of fiscal, monetary and external dealings cannot be achieved, then any commitment the government makes with regard to interest rates, public service charges or exchange rates will be untenable.

The behaviour of prices in the private sector takes in three main areas: those goods and services which make up general consumption; those goods (mainly intermediate goods which are part of the input of the rest of the economy) produced by large firms which constitute a large part of the supply in each sector; and private sector services.

The policy outlined for wages, stabilisation of the prices of variables under public control, and the strategy envisaged for fiscal, monetary and foreign dealings, can only work if the goods and services produced by the private sector are in step with the economic programme as a whole. The success of this programme will depend upon the private sector's voluntary acceptance of the commitments undertaken in the Pact and on the right incentives being offered them (credit and tax incentives, for example). However, at least during the first critical stage when the new economic policy is launched, it will be necessary to establish maximum permissible increases in private sector prices and to provide for controls and sanctions to deal with any infraction, since infractions would undermine any hope of resolving the country's economic crisis and of consolidating its institutional framework. These controls and incentives will be easier to establish for the larger firms, where areas of production and the evolution of costs are verifiable. It will be more difficult in those sectors where there are a large number of suppliers of private goods and in other branches of activity the authorities cannot easily supervise. In the foodstuffs sector, a policy of fixed exchange rates for cereals, meat, and other categories, plus a control on profit margins would enable the government to have considerable influence over price rises.

While the emergency lasts and the commitments made with regard to prices and wages remain in force, it will of course be necessary to make sure that the Pact contains adjustment mechanisms which will help to avoid rigidities that could threaten the necessary redistribution of resources, technological change and capital formation. It will be the success of the stabilising strategy and the fulfillment by the State and the main economic and social agents of the commitments they have undertaken that will later allow prices to stabilise according to a freer play of market forces.

THE PUBLIC SECTOR

Significant changes must be made in the nature of the goods and services offered by the public sector. As capital accumulation stagnated under military rule, so public investment grew more rapidly than private investment. The public investment made was not based on a proper set of priorities (as can be seen for example in the number of urban motorways constructed). This was one of the reasons for the lowering of public sector productivity; that is to say, of the relation between product and capital in the public sector. In addition, the fall in industrial production and in living standards generally has created spare capacity in the existing public sector infrastructure. At the present time, for example, there is spare capacity in the supply of electricity. The available infrastructure must be fully utilised, and a strict list of priorities for public investment programmes worked out. In the next few years, public investment must grow more slowly than private investment. This alteration in the make-up of capital formation, taken together with a better use of infrastructure-capital and of industry's installed capacity, should bring about a considerable improvement in the relation of product to capital.

Expenditure on defence and security, which is difficult to quantify because it is spread throughout almost the whole of the public sector, has grown out of all proportion to the real needs for the defence of national sovereignty and internal security. A limit to the gross volume of all expenditure for defence and security is essential. This limit, if we consider its level in the past and the current desperate economic situation, should be somewhere between 2 and 3 per cent of GDP, that is 20 per cent of the national budget.

This restriction of public investment and defence and security expenditure has as its corollary a necessary improvement in the real wages of State employees, and all those employed in education, health and regional development programmes. There must, therefore, be a considerable modification in the composition of public expenditure.

The current tax structure in Argentina shows an excessive preponderance of regressive taxes over progressive ones, a welter of taxes which add only marginally to the total sum collected (the vast majority of this coming from an extremely reduced number of taxes) and a very high rate of tax evasion, calculated on average as approximately 40 per cent of the nominal tax revenue. These characteristics of our tax system have the most effect on those who earn least. They create high nominal aliquots which punish those who do not evade payment of tax, putting an unfair tax burden on them. They act to inflate the general price level and to discourage investment. A thoroughgoing reform of the tax system is therefore essential, along the following lines:

• An increase in the relative importance of taxes which will make the tax system more progressive;

• A reduction in the number of different taxes in existence, restricting them to those which, at present, account for the main part of the total collected and whose collection cost is less, let us say, than 20 per cent; and,

• Measures which prevent and punish tax evasion and strengthen the operational capacity of the revenue authorities.

Following on from these considerations as to the participation of public expenditure and the tax revenues in the allocation of resources and the distribution of income, the viability of the economic recovery programme, the stability of prices, and the settlement of the foreign debt problem call for the following goals to be met in the public sector:

• A reduction in the participation of total public expenditure in GDP. The aim should be for public expenditure to grow in the years to come at a maximum of 0.8 per cent of GDP;

• Tax revenues (including social contributions) should be kept at 24 per cent of GDP; and,

• The overall public sector debt should be limited to 4 per cent of GDP in 1984, reducing to 2 per cent by 1986.

It is essential that these goals be met if the real wage is to be improved, production revived, inflation checked, and the international payments question settled. They imply an immediate limiting of the public sector's relative weight within the economy, as well as a reduction in its financial imbalance. Above all, they imply the introduction of sweeping changes in both the composition of public expenditure and in the tax payments structure.

The improvement in wages which is an integral part of

the policy described will naturally lead to an increase in expenditure on salaries. The extra money needed to pay for this, plus the extra envisaged for the improvement of health and education services, must be found by reductions in other categories of expenditure. The same will be the case for various subsidies that will be necessary, such as, for example, to help the regions hit by recent natural disasters and, more alarmingly, by the disaster brought upon them by the economic policies of the *de facto* regime. In principle, it appears it will be necessary to reduce expenditure on defence, security and allied costs by about 6 per cent of GDP if these extra costs are to be met. However, since the economy will immediately begin a process of recovery, the necessary savings in real terms will be less than might appear from a simple calculation of the fall in their participation in GDP.

The overall public sector deficit should not be allowed to exceed 4 per cent in 1984, and should then be reduced as we have indicated. As we pointed out in the first part of this book, Argentina's budget situation and balance-of-payments position suggest that it will not be able to pay the outstanding interest on the foreign debt either in 1984 or in the years following even if the aims of the economic programme are met. Consequently, it will be necessary to refinance all the capital repayments and three-quarters of the interest repayments on the foreign public debt over the next few years. The deficit will have to be financed by means of credit from the Central Bank to the Treasury. As we will see later, this monetisation of the fiscal imbalance is compatible with the monetary programme and the other aims outlined for the new economic strategy. The state's domestic debt has already been consolidated following the issue of a long-term bond of 15,000 million Argentine pesos, and has thus ceased to influence the sector's financial position.

As far as the effect of public sector operations on the balance of payments is concerned, it should be noted that the massive increase in military expenditure over recent years and the reliance on imports by those in charge of Argentina's monetarist policies, has led to a substantial increase in the share of public sector imports in total imports.

In addition, the increase in the public foreign debt created a demand for foreign currency to meet the service payments which was impossible given the current situation. As far as the national budget is concerned, there is a limit to the amount which can be transferred abroad. With regard to the other public sector foreign curency expenditure, it is essential to reduce its proportion within total imports to at least the levels of the 1970s. This implies a sizeable reduction in the import of armaments and the strict application, throughout the public sector, of the legislation imposing a 'buy Argentine' policy.

The state enterprises must improve their operating efficiency, and carry out the tariff adjustments previously mentioned while, at the same time, balancing their accounts and restricting the overall imbalance transferable to the Treasury to 1 per cent of GDP. This means that the operating deficit permissible in the state concerns should not exceed 25 per cent of the total envisaged for the whole public sector in 1984. In the years after that, it should fall in line with the anticipated reduction in the fiscal imbalance. If the state concerns cannot be made to adhere to strict policy it will be impossible to achieve the desired goals. That is why these enterprises must be 'nationalised'. That is to say that they must be under strict management control and be supervised by the political institutions of the democratic system. That in itself will not be enough, however. Reforms are also needed in two other main areas. First, a means must be set up whereby the users of public services can complain and bring political pressure to bear in order that the shortcomings and inconsistencies in the provision of these services, and of the goods supplied by state firms, can be eliminated. An institution something like the *ombudsman* which exists in the Scandinavian countries and elsewhere, that is, a powerful representative of the consumers in the political sphere, needs to be established. Secondly, efforts must be made to make the structures of state enterprises more democratic by introducing regulations and criteria which, without affecting operating capacity or the reduc-

tion of costs, will take into account the needs of all the
concerned sectors, including employees and users. A sense
of commitment and participation must be created as an
indispensable prerequisite for the increase of the state firms'
operating efficiency. In short, it is necessary to democratise
the bureaucratic power which, under the military governments, has become rife with privilege, corruption, and
abuses which are incompatible with normal ethical standards of public service and the proper fulfillment of the
responsibilities it has towards the community.

FOREIGN TRADE AND INTERNATIONAL PAYMENTS

In the first three years of this economic programme being
put into practice, there would be a rapid taking up of idle
productive capacity. This would lead to a considerable
increase in imports of primary products and other inputs
needed for domestic economic activity as it recovered. If the
GDP were to grow by 20 per cent between 1984 and 1986,
imports would almost certainly rise by 30 per cent during
the same period. Compared to their depressed 1983 levels
(US$5,000 million by 1986) imports would reach
US$10,000 million. If we suppose that the terms of
international trade remain the same in that time, and that
Argentine exports grow by an annual 6 per cent, then in
1986 the balance of trade surplus would be cut to
US$2,000 million.

Once this three-year period of economic recovery has
been achieved, there must a long-term balance in Argentina's international payments. Given the country's present
level of indebtedness, and the short- and medium-term
prospects of the world financial system and markets, there
is no real possibility of finding external funding to pay for
the balance-of-payments current account deficit (before the
interest on the foreign debt has been paid). The growth of
the Argentine economy will therefore depend to a large
extent on its exporting capacity. From 1987 on, the income
elasticity of exports will have to be at least equal to that of
imports. If we admit that a gradual opening-up of the
Argentine economy will be both a condition for and

evidence of the country's maturity and development, then exports will have to grow approximately 30 per cent more than internal economic activity. Even if this rate can be achieved, and all the more so if exports grow more slowly, a systematic import substitution policy will have to be implemented, together with efforts to integrate Argentina's internal productive activity.

A policy for foreign trade is therefore fundamental to the economic recovery programme and to help to lay solid foundations for the long-term growth of the Argentine economy. In addition, the critical situation in which Argentina finds itself with regard to foreign payments, because of debt servicing, and the need for it to regain autonomy over its own fiscal and monetary policies, means that there must be strict controls to prevent any capital flight and to ensure that foreign currency is used only for essentials.

Argentina must bolster what is its main negotiating strength: its ability to supply all its own essential needs, and the possibility it has to overcome the current crisis and to grow, using its own resources. Argentina's foreign-debt renegotiation must be based on a coherent and firm nationally agreed policy to promote exports, substitute imports, and to ensure that the balance-of-trade current account is regulated. Only then should it undertake foreign-debt interest payments. The imbalance in foreign payments, which is purely financial in origin, should in no way be allowed to affect the development of foreign trade or a normal supply of imported goods and equipment. Argentina has to decide to pay *its own way* using its own resources. Once this political decision has been taken, commercial financing and credit from the industrialised countries is sure to be available, since they need to maintain this credit in order to promote their own exports and domestic economic activity. Argentina must make a clear distinction between the capital and debt interest accounts on one side, and that of productive goods and services on the other. Given the difficulty of the foreign payments situation and the absolute need to pursue a selective imports policy, a National Council for Critical

Imports should be set up. It would comprise both users of imports and members of the appropriate sectors of government, and would work towards avoiding any breakdown in import supplies and to draw up lists of priority items. Above all, it should aim to avoid any build-up of unpaid commercial debts which, if they entailed further supplies being reduced, would have an adverse effect upon Argentina's internal strength, and weaken its foreign negotiating position. This is exactly what the minority who are responsible for the present disaster would like to see happen. They are hoping that the recovery in production can be stifled by a lack of foreign supplies, and that this will lead to debt negotiations in which the orthodox monetarist solution will triumph.

Once such a foreign-trade strategy has been worked out, the limits of how much interest on the foreign debt can be paid will become clear. This strategy will depend on the following basic decisions being taken:

1) *Exchange rate.* A basic exchange rate should be imposed at the level at which it stood at the beginning of 1983. This rate would later be adjusted according to increases in internal prices less the level of inflation internationally. To be effective such a policy would need a rapid decrease in the inflation rate and the successful operation of all the other elements in the proposed strategy.

In order to avoid the effects of the fluctuation of the US dollar against the other major currencies, the rate of the peso should no longer be pegged to the dollar, but should be linked to a basket of currencies such as those which are used to determine the International Monetary Fund's Special Drawing Rights or, alternatively, to an *ad hoc* basket of currencies which would be more representative of the real composition of Argentina's foreign trade. Once this exchange rate had been calculated, the rate of the peso to the dollar and other individual currencies could be worked out.

To avoid problems of over-accounting of imports and under-accounting of exports, changes in the exchange rate should be linked to actual rates; that is, after calculating refunds, import tariffs and deductions. For example, if at the beginning there is a 3 per cent monthly devaluation, the basic exchange rate could rise by 2 per cent with an increase in refunds and tariffs to cover the remaining 1 per cent and a cut in deductions (in order to support the actual rate) of a further 1 per cent. All currency dealings not related to the trade in goods would pay a special tax.

2) *Foreign trade mechanisms.* New mechanisms would be created, and the existing ones strengthened in order to boost exports, open new markets, and diversify exports. Export financing, pre-financing, and guarantees would be reinforced. To encourage new firms from all areas of national life to join in the export effort, special export trading companies would be set up, with the necessary incentives. The exporting capacity of agricultural cooperative would be boosted. The financial aspects of foreign trade would be dealt with by a new Foreign Trade Bank which could be set up, with no new personnel or structures, from the corresponding departments of the National Bank and the other official banks. Argentina's government would seek to promote bilateral agreements and mutual compensation accords with other countries, and in particular would try to strengthen links with Brazil, Argentina's other neighbours, the rest of Latin America, and the developing world in general.

3) *Specific programmes for import substitution.* Argentina's industrial capacity for import substitution, destroyed by the recent free-trade policies, should be restored immediately. There must be incentives for firms which suffered as a result of these free-trade policies to re-establish themselves and to grow. These incentives should be accompanied by the injection of private capital and by modifications to their technology and the structure of their supply to take into account new developments both within Argentina and internationally.

These strict governmental controls over international payments and foreign trade should be kept to the absolute minimum demanded by the emergency in foreign payments and the need to avoid any moves which encourage capital flight. In the short term, exchange controls should be strictly enforced. All the currency gained from exports and other earnings should be channelled through the Central Bank, which should establish a strict list of priorities on how it is to be spent. This list should include essential goods, medical requirements, and foreign-debt payments. Private sector activity in foreign trade, as in other areas of the economy, will be the mainspring for the strengthening of Argentina's international position. Any intervention in the private sector's dealings that is not justified by a defence of the national interest should be avoided.

If the national interest is considered at risk, there should be intervention in private markets and activities without causing any transfer to the public sector, since the latter has shown that it cannot undertake these activities in accordance with the original goals or with a correct evaluation of the public interests at stake. As far as trade in the traditional agricultural products of meat and grains is concerned, the different National Boards must, within the guidelines set out above, exercise a proper supervision of trade flows, avoid any moves which might mean a flight of capital and, in conjunction with private concerns, promote a broadening of markets and a diversification of exports.

As long as there are controls on international payments there is bound to be a parallel exchange market for the peso. It will be insignificant compared to authorised foreign-trade transactions and financial dealings. It can, however, have an important negative effect on the climate of opinion which it creates among economic agents and in giving impetus to the flight of capital through mechanisms relating to foreign-trade prices. The first way of dealing with this situation is to make sure that the suggested controls, which were all but dismantled under the monetarist ministers, work properly. Beyond this, the coherence of the government's overall economic strategy must be obvious to everyone. If a viable exchange rate policy can be maintained, together with a lending rate that does not lead to capital flight, and fiscal and monetary policies which act together to aid economic recovery and price stability, the gap between the official exchange rate and the parallel one can be kept within manageable limits.

CURRENCY AND CREDIT

Argentina must regain autonomy over its monetary policies, which have been submitted, since the installation of military regimes in 1976, to the opinions of economic agents as to the relative advantages of financial assets held in pesos or in foreign currency. This has meant that the general interest level and the internal liquidity rate were dependent on exchange rates and the country's international reserves position. With funds able to move freely, and within the context of the so-called 'monetarist view of the balance of payments', any discrepancy between the domestic interest rate and supply of credit and the expectations of these economic agents was immediately reflected in a drop in international reserves. The situation was controlled by reducing internal liquidity and a rise in the interest rate. This was the method adopted after 1976, when the transfer of funds abroad was made progressively freer, and the interest rate was allowed to be dictated by the market. At present, it is the exchange rate on the parallel market which determines monetary policy and sets the limits of credit expansion, despite the existence of controls on the movement of funds outside the country.

As things now stand, any recovery plan for the Argentine economy is impossible. It is therefore essential to separate monetary policy from the foreign-debt situation, and to discuss debt payments on completely different terms. To separate the interest rate and the supply of credit from these restricting external factors, a strict exchange control must be brought in which would deny the economic agents the choice of whether to hold their financial assets in pesos or foreign currency. In other words, there must be effective controls which oblige those people with savings or financial assets either to acquire productive assets or to keep their holdings in pesos.

As we have already noted, a policy of this kind will only be successful if the government's overall economic policy is coherent and if a climate of confidence in the growth and stability of the Argentine economy can be created. This coherence can only be achieved if there is a unified leadership in charge of fiscal, monetary, and balance-of-payments policy. Consequently, at least for as long as the current emergency lasts, the same official should head the Ministry of Economy and the Central Bank. Day-to-day problems could be solved by an under-secretary for monetary affairs and external payments, attached to the Ministry of Economics, who would at the same time have administrative charge of the Central Bank. It would be for the government to establish the level of credit available and the interest rate. The former would be determined according to a precisely worked-out programme of financing for both the private and public sectors. There is little hope that in the first years after the adoption of this policy there would be sufficient improvement in the international reserves position to finance monetary expansion. The government could seek to use its monetary policies to compensate for this. An expansion of credit and the money supply which would not endanger economic recovery or the stability of prices would depend on an increase in production and in real income, and a demand for money by the public matched by the rate of monetisation.

These two factors are interrelated. The growth of real income and of production generates a greater demand for money for transactions, and a greater level of savings held by individuals, which could be used as financial assets. However, the demand for money is also conditioned by the profitability of these assets. To expand the demand for money, the borrowing rate must be sufficiently high to encourage savers. In this way, the money supply can be increased without affecting prices. Given the very low current level of monetisation (approximately 12 per cent in Argentina), this could be stepped up if the interest rate were dealt with as suggested, and, above all, if inflation were cut drastically and money once again had deposit value.

The government should also fix the borrowing and lending rates. These rates should take into account the effect they will have on the demand for money and their relation to the profitability of firms' investments. The real annual lending rate should not be above 5 per cent and must remain stable.* The instability and disproportionately high level of real lending rates during the seven years of military government should not provoke a return to heavily negative rates, which would act to depress monetisation, the availability of resources, and do nothing to solve the problem of inflation.

To fix the borrowing rate, the government should allow a maximum spread of only 0.8 per cent monthly as the cost of financial dealings. It would have to pay close attention to the operations of financial institutions to avoid any manoeuvres that would increase the spread by increasing the interest rate actually paid by recipients of credit. As part of its overall programme, the government should decide if this level of spread is completely absorbed by the borrowing rate or if there is to be some means of partly subsidising it. If the latter were the case, this subsidy should be part of the public sector's overall deficit and its effect on the monetary strategy should be quantified.

The existence of a fixed interest rate might lead to speculative operations between different types of financial holdings. This will be a risk if the rate is set too far below what can be obtained by other financial dealings; and this, in turn, happens if the rate of inflation is not brought down to levels compatible with the aims of the monetary policy. But the same may also happen if there are credit bonds which offer security and liquidity and therefore give rise to speculative dealings. This will influence the policies of an open market and public financing. Naturally, it is also essential to supervise the emission of fixed-rate credits.

The government should regulate this credit by means of a 100 per cent or fractionary reserve. The bank rate will be set in accordance with the overall priorities of the economic programme. There would be no room for an institutionalised free money market. However, in practice, a parallel money market with a free interest rate would probably

---

* In order for this rate to apply not only to the major firms, the Central Bank will ensure that part of its loans to the commercial banks is reserved exclusively for small- and medium-sized companies.

grow up. The behaviour of this unofficial sector could be useful as an indicator of market trends, and the government would have the ways and means to keep control over it.

The system would operate with an official guarantee for 100 per cent of deposits and payable interest. The number of financial companies in existence would be cut, and the number of their subsidiaries would be frozen for a minimum five-year period. These financial intermediaries grew out of all proportion under military rule. This has created a further problem, a social one this time, for of the 15,000 people employed in the financial sector, approximately one-third would be made redundant in any rationally planned, efficient financial system. This factor should be taken into account when any reorganisation is carried out. The employees of these companies should not be made responsible for the consequences of the speculative rush which characterised the monetarist period of the Argentine economy.

The official banking system has to recover its decisive role in the functioning of the financial system, and must undergo a thorough overhaul. The number of institutions should be reduced, and at the same time strengthened. The provincial banks should be grouped together in large regional entities. Rather than continue to open new branches as they have done since 1976, the official banks should try to reduce their number, or to transfer them to more appropriate bodies.

No new foreign banks should be allowed to establish themselves in Argentina, nor should any more national banks be bought by foreign ones already operating in the country. There must be an indefinite ban on foreign banks opening new branches; they should only be permitted to relocate and rationalise their existing ones. Of the thirty-two foreign banks now operating, sixteen were set up in Argentina following the 1977 Financial Reform. Most of these banks were never firmly established, and only function to offer large loans and for foreign-currency dealings. The policy we are proposing would restrict the role of these foreign banks to external financing operations.

All the financial institutions would be governed by universal banking regulations. In today's Argentina, there is no real place for any narrowly specialised financial body. Those authorised to operate should therefore be allowed to do so over the whole range of financial services.

The Central Bank's inspectorate should keep a close watch on these financial institutions. It should ensure that the norms of solvency, liquidity, and efficiency are strictly adhered to. There should be a tightening up of the regulations which oblige all bodies not fulfilling official requirements to do so in as short a time as possible. It would be useful to set a maximum operating limit according to the amount of pesos deposited, and for institutions which did not respect this limit to be called on to work out ways of complying with it as soon as possible.

It is worth noting, finally, that the consolidation and debt refinancing plan brought in by the 1982 Reform has now been overtaken by events. Total private financial sector debts stand at around 55,000 million Argentine pesos. They could be refinanced over five years (with monthly repayments) with a one-year grace period at the agreed interest rate.

MEASURES AGAINST EXTREME POVERTY

The economic recovery programme should include specific provisions to help to alleviate the extreme poverty from which a considerable proportion of Argentina's inhabitants are suffering, and which the economic decline of recent years has made even worse. Any such measures would have to deal with two basic causes of poverty: unemployment and the below subsistence-level income of many members of both the working and non-working population. These problems will be solved in time by the country's economic recovery, and the increase in employment and real wages. However, the most urgent problems need to be dealt with immediately, and specific policies designed to combat poverty must be worked out.

As far as employment is concerned, financial and fiscal incentives must be given to those firms which employ workers paid at the bottom end of the wage scale. The Central Bank should, as part of its overall strategy for bolstering monetary resources, establish certain discount credits for this category of firm. The government tax system should include concessions for firms which employ people from among the pool of unemployed or the poorly paid. There should also be special schemes for young persons going out to work for the first time. These would revolve around redundancy payments (which the state could pay either in whole or in part) and the introduction of a graduated scale of redundancy payments to discourage people from voluntarily leaving jobs. The government has a wide range of possibilities open to it to help boost employment and productivity.

The minimum wage must be raised from its current level of 25 per cent of basic consumer needs. This could be achieved by implementing the financial and tax schemes already mentioned. Increases in pensions should be weighted to give more assistance to those most in need. At present there is too great a discrepancy between those retired people on a minimum pension and those who enjoy special schemes. Any changes should link pensions to the minimum wage, and a proportionally greater increase should be awarded to those on the lower grades, as well as to the most elderly.

Argentina's current social security system and the Ministry of Social Welfare do have programmes designed to meet the needs of the poorest sectors of society. These are insufficient, and need to be improved and extended. School-age children should be cared for with the introduction of special food aid at their schools, even on days when they do not have to attend, and during holidays. In proven cases of need, the children should be given their school uniforms, books, and shoes free of charge. It has been found that an important factor in family poverty is the low level of economic activity of those members other than the head of the household who have to look after the younger children. Although it is obviously desirable to safeguard family unity, since this is vital to a child's proper development, there should be provision for more crèches and nurseries, which would guarantee some formal education to the children and free other members of the family for remunerative work. Family allowances must also be raised: at present they are some 80 per cent lower in real terms than they were in 1970.

Health and food problems demand further measures. The provision of rebates on prescriptions for retired people and through social security provisions should be extended to the unemployed and to those with low earnings. Food stamps might also be issued to the unemployed, thus ensuring for them at least a minimum food intake. Self-employed people could be dealt with through the Self-Employed Savings Bank. Food stamps would be only for the most basic items, and would cover either all or part of the cost. It would be for the State to compile a list of such basic items and to make sure that private firms supplied them at reduced cost. These firms would be compensated by the guarantee of a large and predictable market.

All these schemes will, of course, depend on the resources available, the overall situation of the public sector, and the income redistribution made possible by the economic recovery, fuller employment, and higher real wages.

SELF-FINANCING INVESTMENT PROJECTS

Several areas, particularly those related to the country's infrastructure and its basic industries, are suitable for projects which could pay for themselves once they have got under way. The projects include some imported inputs (which could be paid for by external financial and supply credits) and expenditure within Argentina for such items as the labour force, materials, equipment, and so on. Under the system of conceding leases for the building of public works, at present it is the State which acts as guarantor for all this investment, and basically finances the projects from public resources. This was the case with the motorways and other public works projects carried out during the military regimes. These projects did not involve any real private investment. We now have to work out a different system; one which does not imply an official guarantee, but which offers the private sector a major role in carrying out the schemes which are a priority if Argentina's economy is to return to growth.

In the current international situation, foreign contractors and suppliers of equipment are obviously interested in taking part in the large-scale public works projects planned in Argentina, such as the Paraná hydroelectric scheme, and the nuclear power station programme. The same is true in the gas and oil industries. The private sector has plans to convert gas into liquid fuel and for transforming and exporting hydrocarbons. One of the traditional ways for the private sector to invest involves private risk capital, where the investment made is recouped by means of the activity financed. There could also be special incentives for the repatriation of capital held abroad by Argentine residents. This would be linked to the financing and implementation of investment projects.

The Social and Economic Pact should include a series of self-financing projects of this kind, which would permit a considerable volume of investment without the draining of official resources or domestic credit. Finance for the local part of these schemes would be provided by private risk capital whether in pesos or in foreign currency. In the latter case, the foreign funds made available would also lead to the creation of Argentine money. This is the kind of situation we were referring to when, talking of foreign debt, we stated that the inflow of funds for investment projects could be a way of compensating for the temporary lack of sources of financial credit.

Another way of helping to finance such projects would be to reintroduce the National Development Fund, to which the working population could contribute and which would be administered by the National Development Bank (in conjuction with other public bodies such as the National Mortgage Bank). Contributions to this fund could be calculated as the equivalent to so many hours work per month. This amount could be adjusted according to the official interest rate, and would be immediately convertible if an emergency should arise, with the guarantee of additional credits if need be.

The change in the international situation and the consolidation in Argentina of a representative regime which, by definition, will defend its own national interest, will modify the political position and the terms for negotiating with foreign firms. As part of the expansion of the Argentine economy and the plans for each sector, foreign subsidiaries in Argentina must be encouraged to step up their investments and business. Priority should be given to those schemes that increase employment, help the development of import substitutes, generate exports, decentralise production and promote technological development. There should also be negotiations with other foreign firms interested in helping in different areas of Argentina's development and in the consolidation of a democratic regime which will provide the institutional stability that can offer long-term guarantees for foreign investors. These firms' investments should be directed to areas which will provide a real stimulus for development. Once democracy has been firmly re-established in Argentina and the economic recovery has become a fact, the country will attract many foreign investors. They will be able to contribute (though in a small proportion compared to the capital formation provided by national savings) to the overall increase in investments. Given the large numbers of multinational companies now operating, a representative government in Argentina will, as part of a comprehensive nationalist plan, negotiate on very different terms from the past. The government will be able to negotiate technology transfers, the balance of currency held by the companies, the participation of national and foreign capital; in short, all those factors which can help to balance the interests of the private foreign investor with those of the country concerned. Room for manoeuvre exists in this respect, as long as the government negotiates with national interests at heart rather than those of the minority which supports the multinationals. Since 1976, and in earlier experiences, we have seen quite plainly that this minority, by reducing the level of economic activity, drives out foreign investment and lessens the interest of foreign investors in participating in Argentina's development. Naturally, the change in

Argentina's political circumstances will also help to create favourable conditions for the repatriation of capital held abroad by Argentine residents.

The recovery of Argentina's regional economies and that of its different productive sectors calls for a concerted effort by both the public and the private sectors. The Economic and Social Pact should provide the framework for the following steps to be taken:

1) *Sectoral agreements in manufacturing industry.* Commissions should be set up to study the conversion and expansion of the different branches of industry (textiles, machine-tools, meat-packing, food, etc) so that the necessary aid can be given to the private sector. These commissions would seek agreement as to how the firms (by increasing capital etc) and the public sector (by means of credits, export incentives, etc) could best help to modernise, to increase the scale of production, to improve technology levels and that of equipment, to launch them on the international market, and, if need be, to provide for mergers. These commissions would comprise representatives from the firms involved, their work-forces, and the State. Each of them would have an administration in which the Ministry of Industry and other relevant public departments would be included. Within six months of their establishment, these commissions should set out practical proposals which could be incorporated into the Economic and Social Pact.

2) *Agreements on the regional economies.* Argentina's regions have been badly hit by the recent monetarist policies, which have served to worsen still further their traditional structural problems of rigidities in supply, dependency on the metropolitan region, and so on. Each region ought to put forward specific recovery programmes based on proposals from the provincial governments, and from representatives of firms based in the region, their work-forces

and the national State. These programmes would cover such matters as how to improve exports, the creation of centres of development, the reconversion of industries, and the extension of agricultural land. They would be coordinated within the Pact at the national level, and would therefore lead to the adoption of a coherent package of measures designed to promote the development and resources of each region. These regional schemes would mean that the large infrastructural projects currently completed or planned (such as Chocón, Salto Grande, or Yacyretá) would become focal points for regional development rather than merely being the source of energy supplies for the metropolitan region.

3) *Agreements for the agricultural sector.* Agricultural development of the fertile *pampas* and the extension of exploitable land in the rest of Argentina could give an important boost to agricultural production. Under the terms of the Economic and Social Pact, agreement would be sought between organisations representing the producers, the rural workers, and the State, as to specific ways of bringing about technological change, capitalisation of agricultural enterprises, the diversification and more efficient rotation of crops, and the extension of workable land. Administration of this process would be the responsibility of the relevant bodies in the public sector (the Ministry of Agriculture, the National Institute of Agricultural Technology).

4) *Schemes for small- and medium-sized firms.* Even in the largest industrialised countries, this category comprises the most dynamic and profitable segment of productive activity. Technological advances being made now, and the ability of these firms to respond to changes in patterns of demand, and the diversification of markets, make it necessary to work out specific measures for them to develop their own technology, to increase their capitalisation, and break into the international market. A special commission for this purpose would be set up under the Economic and Social Pact, to offer them support. The firms themselves, their work-forces, and the relevant state bodies would all be

represented. It would be the Ministry of Industry's task to oversee the administration of this commission.

5) *Housing.* The present housing shortage in Argentina, together with the importance of the construction industry for the economy as a whole make the adoption of a nationwide building programme essential. This would also be part of the Pact, and its details would be worked out by a commission made up of the relevant professional bodies, building firms and the appropriate technical organisations. The National Mortgage Bank could coordinate and administer this programme.

6) *The privatisation and relaunching of idle companies.* Even prior to the April 1980 financial crisis, many firms had come under state control because of the disastrous effects of the policies followed after April 1976. Most of these firms are currently controlled by the Central Bank, which, when it wound up the affairs of different financial institutions, took over their assets. Many of them are potentially viable concerns, and should be relaunched as quickly as possible, being at the same time transferred back to the private sector. After consulting all the groups and interests involved, the regulations governing this transfer to the private sector should be speedily established, so that these companies can become productive again, or, if this proves impossible, so that their assets can be realised as soon as possible. There should be a plan detailing how (by the capitalisation of banking debts, fresh inputs of capital, and so on) these firms can be transferred to responsible private groups, with the aim of being scrupulously impartial and of defending the public interest.

12

The macroeconomic factors

OVERALL SUPPLY AND DEMAND

Taking into account the Argentine economy's behaviour in the past, the present situation and the policies proposed, the following changes in the main variables are to be expected for the three years 1984–6:

- Real wages: an increase of 30 per cent.
- Elasticity of consumption/GDP: 1.
- Savings rate/GDP: 20 per cent.
- Marginal output/capital ratio: 3.15*
- Elasticity of employment/GDP: 0.4
- Elasticity of imports/GDP: 1.4

If the proposed policies are put into effect, there should be a rapid recovery in both production and employment. The present imbalances, together with the balance-of-payments restrictions and obstacles which are likely to occur in the re-allocation of resources and in income redistribution, lead one to the conclusion that the growth rate will not be any more rapid than that experienced on previous occasions when Argentina's economy made a spectacular recovery. The policies to boost demand and production must therefore be as bold as possible and take full account of the real available resources, as well as the constraints of the present situation. Once this basic assumption has been accepted, the proposed policies would allow the production targets shown in Table 1 to be met.

* According to calculations by J Sourrouille, the marginal output/capital ratio will be low during the stages of an economic recovery following a recession. In the 1959–61 recovery, the rate was 2.5, and with a savings coefficient of 18 per cent, output grew at an annual rate of 7.2 per cent. In the 1963–6 economic recovery, with a rate of 3.0 and a savings coefficient of 18 per cent of GDP, output grew by an annual 6.7 per cent.

Table 1
Overall supply and demand 1984–6
(percentage increase)

	Total		Annual rate
Overall supply	20.7	(100)*	6.5
GDP	20.1	(91)	6.3
Imports	27.7	(9)	8.5
Overall demand	20.7	(100)	6.5
Consumption	24.2**	(71)	7.5
Investment	19.4	(14)	6.1
Exports	6.0	(15)	2.0

* The numbers in brackets represent the participation of each item in overall supply and demand. ** Including the effect of greater participation by wage-earners.

Table 2
Gross domestic product by sector 1984–6
(percentage increase)

	Total	Annual rate
Industry	25.2	7.8
Agriculture	10.0	3.2
Construction	25.2	7.8
Services	19.1	6.0
TOTAL	20.1	6.3

It is to be hoped that the economic recovery will take place mainly in the goods-producing sector, and in particular in manufacturing industry, where there is most idle productive capacity, and where the improvement in purchasing power would be most felt. Taking into account the past experience in Argentina with regard to input-output, the growth of the different economic sectors would be as represented in Table 2.

EMPLOYMENT AND INCOME DISTRIBUTION

If these targets for economic growth are achieved, and the elasticity of income for employment proves well-founded,

Table 3
Economically active population 1983–6
(in thousands)

	1983	1986	Annual rate of increase
Total population	29,000	30,300	1.5
Economically active population	11,300	12,200	2.6
Wage-earners	8,250	9,150	2.9
Non wage-earners	3,050	3,050	0.0

then there would be an increase of 90,000 jobs between 1984 and 1986. If this were so, it is to be expected that the increase would be due above all to an expansion in the number of wage-earners rather than in the non-wage-earning population, which would remain at similar levels to 1983. Table 3 details the evolution of the economically active population between 1983 and 1986 and its composition.

The share of the economically active population with respect to the total will grow from 39 per cent in 1983 to 40.4 for the three years 1984–6. The percentage of wage-earners in the total economically active population will increase from 73 per cent to 75 per cent in the same years. These developments are consistent with the changes that can be expected from the country's economic recovery and will correct the distortions that grew up in the years 1976–83 because of economic stagnation, the crisis in manufacturing industry, the boom in self-employment and the disproportionate growth in the non-active population.

The increase in employment and in real wages forecast in these tables is also consistent. If real wages increase by 30 per cent over the three years from 1984–6 and wage earners by 8 per cent, the payments to wages will grow by 40 per cent over the three years. The increase in GDP will be 20.1 per cent. If the wage-earners account for 35 per cent of national income in 1983, this increase in wages will take their participation to 40.4 per cent by 1986. This increase is compatible with the other aims of the economic recovery programme. Non-wage income will grow by 10.3 per cent in the 1983–6 period which is consistent with the expected evolution of private investment and tax revenues. In other words, the income redistribution proposed is compatible with the economic recovery with external payments, capital formation and the anti-inflationary measures proposed in the economic programme.

FOREIGN TRADE AND INTERNATIONAL PAYMENTS

Export forecasts for the three years 1984–6 are based on the following assumptions:

1) *Agricultural products.* The elasticity of aggregate consumption with regard to agricultural products is calculated at 1.0 for beef, 0.7 for other meat products, and 0.4 for cereals. Given the rates of overall growth estimated and the participation of agriculture in that total, the growth of domestic consumption of agricultural products will be in the order of 14.5 per cent. Since the estimated total increase of agricultural production is 10 per cent, the physical output of agricultural exports will grow 1.7 per cent between 1983 and 1986 (0.5 per cent annually).

2) *Industrial goods* (other than those of agricultural origin). They comprise 30 per cent of total exports, and should grow by 16 per cent between 1983 and 1986 (5 per cent per year).

This increase in agricultural and industrial exports would allow an increase of exportable output of 2 per cent per year (6 per cent over the three years). Once full employment has been achieved from 1986 onwards, there should be a narrowing of the gap between the growth rates of exports and imports. We have assumed that the terms of trade will remain substantially the same as those operative in 1983. We are expecting an elasticity of income for the import of goods of the order of 1.4. This would mean an increase of 26 per cent between 1983 and 1986 (at an annual rate of 8 per cent over the three years 1984–6). As far as productive services are concerned (freight, tourism, etc) both exports and imports should register an elasticity of

Table 4
Balance of payments 1983–6
(in millions of US dollars)

	1983	1984	1985	1986
Exports	8,500	9,300	10,100	11,100
Imports	−5,500	−6,400	−7,400	−8,600
Trade balance	3,000	2,900	2,700	2,500
Services	−500	−500	−500	−500
Interest	−5,500	−5,200	−5,600	−6,100
Current Account	−2,500	−2,800	−3,400	−4,100
Capital	2,500	3,500	4,000	4,500
Change in reserves	—	700	600	400
Foreign debt	41,500	45,000	49,000	53,500

1.4, with an annual deficit of US$500 million over the period in question. International export and import prices are expected to grow at 7 per cent annually.

Maximum repayment of interest on the foreign debt should be 10 per cent of exports, and we estimate that the average interest rate on the foreign debt (including surcharge, commission, etc) will be approximately 12.5 per cent annually. A renegotiation of the existing foreign debt would allow the amortisation periods to be extended, although a rapid consolidation of the debt is thought unlikely.

On the basis of these assumptions, Table 4 sets out the expected balance-of-payments situation for 1983–6.

As can be seen, according to these assumptions, the foreign debt would increase from US$41,000 in 1983 to US$53,500 million in 1986. In real terms, if one deducts estimated international inflation for that period, the debt in 1986 would be approximately US$45,000 million. Its composition could change, however, as external finance came to include supply credits to provide import capital to pay for the investment programmes envisaged in the economic recovery plan. This would mean that the part of the debt that is owed to private foreign banks (some 70 per cent of the total in 1983) could be reduced.

The forecasts in Table 4 show that the surplus on the

Table 5

	1984	1985	1986
1. Current Resources	35	36	37
Tax revenues	21	22	23
Non-tax revenues	14	14	14
2. Current expenditure	29	29	28
Salaries	10	10	10
Goods, services and others	19	19	18
3. Savings (1−2)	6	7	9
4. Investment	9	9	10
5. Deficit (4−3)	3	2	1
6. Interest	5	5	5
7. Finance (5+6)	8	7	6
Central Bank	4	3	2
External Credit	4	4	4

balance of trade less the increase in foreign reserves for the 1984–6 period will reach US$6,400 million, equivalent to 21 per cent of exports over the same period. They indicate therefore that, given a firm line on renegotiating the foreign debt, Argentina has ample room for manoeuvre in its international relations.

THE PUBLIC SECTOR

Table 5 shows the evolution of the consolidated public sector consistent with the proposed policies.

THE MONETARY SECTOR

In order to ensure that the evolution of the monetary sector is consistent with the policies that have been put forward in this book, the performance of key variables can be seen according to various assumptions about the inflation rate. The assumptions behind the calculations are that, at the start of the new policy, the principal relations are: M2/GDP is 10 per cent; M1/M2* is 40 per cent, and the balance of credit between the public and private sectors is 35 per cent

* M1 corresponds to banknotes and coins held by the public plus demand deposits; M2 is M1 plus time deposits.

and 65 per cent of the total. We are also estimating for the 1984–6 period a spread between borrowing and lending rates of 7 per cent annually. We further estimate a 3 per cent increase in credit to the private sector from the initial stock of credit to finance the wage increases scheduled for the start of the economic recovery programme. The credit stock for the private sector would increase an annual 10 per cent during the three years, 1984–6. The public sector deficit would be 4 per cent of GDP in 1984, 3 per cent in 1985, and 2 per cent in 1986. It has also been assumed that the interest rate for loans will equal the rate of inflation.

With a monthly inflation rate of 3 per cent (42.5 per cent annually), the aforementioned assumptions will imply a growth of M2 of 110 per cent in 1984, 77 per cent in 1985, and 64 per cent in 1986. Given that the estimated increase in real GDP will be an annual 6.3 per cent for 1984–6, it can be seen that the liquidity coefficient (M2/GDP) will have grown (at the end of each year) by 10 per cent in 1983, 13.9 per cent in 1984, 16.3 per cent in 1985, and 17.6 per cent in 1986. It should also be noted that the share of the public sector in M2 growth will drop from 45 per cent of the total in 1984 to 32 per cent in 1985 and 22 per cent in 1986. This is assuming that the external sector will have no repercussions on the monetary sector.

This increase in liquidity, including the 3 per cent monthly inflation rate, is considerable, and would imply a proportionate increase in the general demand for financial assets. This could be met if the democratic government becomes firmly established and coherent economic policies produce a favourable change in the climate of economic opinion and help stimulate financial savings. A real loan interest rate of zero might be sufficient to encourage private savings in financial assets.

Of course, the rhythm of monetary expansion will be conditioned by the fiscal deficit. Any increase in the money supply depends to a large extent on the reduction of this deficit and the restriction of the increase of credit to the private sector to limits compatible with the growth of overall liquidity in the system. The fiscal deficit and its effect on the monetary sector are also brakes on how far the inflation rate can be reduced. If, with the same assumptions as we made previously, we estimate that the monthly inflation rate is in the region of 4.5 per cent in 1984, 4 per cent in 1985, and 3.5 per cent in 1986, the coefficient of liquidity will grow less than it would according to the assumption of an average 3 per cent monthly increase in inflation for the whole period 1984–6. The relation M2/GDP would grow from 13 per cent in 1984 to 14.7 per cent in 1985, and 15.8 per cent in 1986.

These estimates serve to show how important a planned monetary sector is for the Economic and Social Pact and for the economic recovery policy and also demonstrate the consistency of the policies put forward in this book.